Get Off the Bench and Get in the Game

Vital Behaviors for Success in Life and dōTERRA

By Justin Harrison

D1124732

Get Off The Bench and Get In The Game

Vital Behaviors for Success in Life and dōTERRA

Printed in the United States of America

ISBN 978-0-692-33670-0

Second Edition

Published by MyOilBusiness

www.myoilbusiness.com

Produced by Scottsdale Multimedia, Inc.

Earnings Disclaimer:

The ideas and concepts within this book are designed to provide readers with the encouragement, strategies and motivation necessary to build a successful business in the profession of network marketing. It is understood by the reader, that your results are based on your own individual efforts, abilities and work ethic.

Table of Contents

● ● ●

Introduction

I experienced an inner revolution at a fairly young age. It was a form of enlightenment for me, a fundamental shift in the way I saw potential and possibility both for my own future and for the future of others around me.

It was 1996, and I was in Cache Valley, Utah studying in the engineering program at Utah State University. Up to that point I had always wanted to build something great but even though I got an A in the introductory engineering class, I quickly discovered that engineering just wasn't capturing my interests.

After that experience, I changed my major to business thinking I could build something lasting that way. By that time, however, I was like most college students: broke and hungry. Living off macaroni and cheese was getting old quickly, so I decided to get a job.

Of course this was before the Internet days so I turned to the best source at the time for available jobs: the newspaper. I saw an ad there inviting people to interview for a new business opportunity. I was studying business anyway, so I was intrigued and called the number.

What I experienced was nothing like a traditional job interview. I went to downtown Logan where two ladies had reserved an office with a little training room. The interview itself was really more of a formal presentation for a company that has since gone out of business. I wasn't told about a job; I was told about an opportunity to build a business of my own.

These women opened my eyes to an alternative way of earning a living. The traditional career model is to earn an income through 100 percent of your own efforts (after taxes, of course). I knew and understood that model. My parents had lived that model. These women put forth the idea that I could earn a very small percentage (1 percent or so) of the efforts of a large group of people instead, possibly thousands of people. It wasn't hard for me to do that math and see the scope of what they were suggesting, and I liked what I saw.

Some people might have shied away from the idea of running a business and being their own boss — especially at such a young age — but I didn't. My family background had instilled in me some entrepreneurial, independent, provident-living principles, and I saw a way to live those principles through this opportunity. I also saw a way to take greater control of my own life and where it would lead. So I bit.

Family Background

The courage to take the bait came from some of the preparation of my childhood. Let me share some of the entrepreneurial, independent-thinking principles I learned from my family upbringing. An event that occurred when I was about 12 years old is one of the pivotal experiences that helped instill these principles in me at an early age. My dad came home one day and announced that the mortgage on the house was paid in full. Now, my dad wasn't some rich corporate executive, and he didn't discover oil or gold in the backyard either. He was a police officer and my mom was a homemaker. Both are noble professions, but we all know that neither one pays that much money. Still, on such meager wages, they had paid off the house. In addition and to their credit, my mom and dad were only in their early 30s at that point.

Of course, the house cost a lot less than a house costs nowadays (maybe $20,000 or $30,000 instead of the $200,000 to $300,000 a starter home can cost today), so the house payments were comparatively lower. But we were still a single-income family living on policeman wages, so our income was relatively low as well. My parents were just very aware of their finances, and they made double or triple house payments each month, saving an enormous amount of interest.

When you stick to a plan like that over time, it results in a free-and-clear home in far less than the banks' 30-year target. So, at age 12, I learned the value of careful financial planning and management. The lessons didn't stop there.

Resourcefulness and entrepreneurism were additional lesson I learned in my parents' home. My dad was something of a mountain man and would go into the mountains and trap wild game, skin the animals, and sell the furs. A bobcat pelt could go for as much as $700 in today's dollars. If he could trap 50 or so of those animals, he knew he could bring in a significant amount of money. And with low policeman wages trying to pay off the house in half the usual amount of time, every little bit helped.

On top of that, my parents would run a fireworks stand every summer around the Fourth of July, bringing home a piece of that seasonal industry. The point is that my parents weren't content to just sit and draw a policeman's salary; they were always looking for opportunities and ways to make additional money.

Their example has influenced me throughout my life. They are the reason I learned that careful financial management can lead to financial freedom on almost any income — no matter how small. I also learned that it's better to be paid for one's results, rather than one's time or effort. Punching a clock is no way to really get ahead in life — though it can certainly keep you afloat.

My parents weren't afraid to be their own bosses — though my dad certainly had a boss and a chain of command in connection with his work as a police officer. In their side businesses, however, my parents were responsible only to themselves. I saw that example and learned that it was okay to be your own boss.

My parents never aspired to be corporate executives and have a private jet or anything like that. Instead, their humble, quiet example taught me a different view of success and how to achieve it — a view that made me very open to what the two women in the downtown Logan office were pitching in 1996 to a hungry, broke college student.

MLM Company

I recognized during my university days that I could go the traditional route and get into a business somewhere and be very successful that way. People do it all the time, and I say good for them. I think that's great but also realized that these women were offering me a different-but-equally-valid path to get to success. I didn't see it as a get-rich-quick scheme either. This was a way to legitimately focus my efforts, channel my talents, and earn a good living.

Comparing the two ways of making a living, it was obvious that it's better to earn a fraction of a percent of an army of people than to do the equivalent amount of work myself. It clicked, and I wanted in.

Interestingly, and as you may have recognized, their offer was a chance to join an MLM, or a multilevel marketing company. Most people in America run in any other direction when they hear the MLM pitch, but I was totally oblivious to the concept – I had never heard of it before.

Although my parents had instilled invaluable principles within me, their mentoring came with no specific plan for my path to success. They hadn't ever gone down the "networking marketing" path (network marketing is what MLM is generally called within the industry today). Additionally, the profession itself was still fairly young. Over the next few years, several network marketing companies made headlines with their lavish parties and lifestyles, but I hadn't been exposed to any of that yet. I'd hardly even heard of Amway, beyond the fact that it existed. I had no concept of how a network marketing company was structured or how the pay scale worked or anything else but I was willing to learn.

The MLM's product was a line of dietary supplements, but that didn't really matter to me. I was sold on the idea of being my own boss and being able to multiply my own efforts through a team of, potentially, hundreds or thousands of other people. I was less concerned about the product. In my eyes, that was just a vehicle, a method of movement. I saw the value in the structure of the company and didn't just get involved after that... I swallowed the bait, hook, line, and sinker all the way down to my toes. I jumped in with an almost reckless abandon and fully immersed myself in the concept of network marketing and the networking profession. I bit so hard that when I found out the company didn't really have a presence in my hometown of Idaho Falls, Idaho I moved back home. It was only a couple months after my initial meeting with those two women, and I was ready to break open a new area and build out my network. I was ready to go to work.

Getting Started

I started out by making contacts and invitations to come to an introductory event I was setting up. I reserved a space at an awful, rundown recreation center in Idaho Falls. The center was right on the river, and the meeting room only cost me $20 to reserve for the evening. I suppose I should have seen all those things as red flags, but I was too impassioned to notice. This was back before the days of PowerPoint, so I had to do all my visuals on an overhead projector and a chalkboard. We didn't even have dry-erase boards at that point.

I arrived early and set up a really nice product display and got everything ready. I had invited my parents and a bunch of their friends to come and give me a chance to present. I was still new at the whole thing, so I thought it would be wise to start close to home. I thought that would be safer than starting with total strangers.

By 6:45 p.m., no one had shown up. The meeting wasn't supposed to start until 7:00 anyway, so I wasn't particularly worried yet, but I had to start considering the possibilities. I stayed patient as the clock passed 6:50, then 6:55, until it reached 7:00. I still didn't have a single warm body in the room with me and I started to do what's called "the walk." The walk is when you check around the conference room, go up the hall and peek out into the parking lot, then hurry back to the room to make sure you don't miss anyone. I did that until about 7:15, at which point I finally realized that no one was coming. Not even my parents. My first event on my own and it was a no show. I sat down and looked at my product display and said to myself, "Well, that's a sweet product display." Then I packed it up and went home.

Everyone had their reasons for not being there, of course, and I don't remember any of those reasons now, but it was very discouraging all the same. It would have been really easy to quit at that point, and I think many people would have. Around that same time, I realized that I must have been one of the only people in the world who didn't know what a network marketing company was all about, or at least the only one who didn't *think* he knew what they were about. Shortly after moving home, I started to learn the popular public sentiment about companies like mine. I started to hear terms like "MLM" and "pyramid scheme." In fact, I had an aunt who had made it her mission in life to antagonize me about the whole opportunity. I loved her to pieces, but for months and months her first question to me when we would meet was always something along the lines of "Have you made any money yet?" This didn't stop me. When I signed up, I knew I was signing up for something difficult. It was a simple concept on paper but I knew it wouldn't be easy in practice, so I was ready for the hardship and I kept going. I kept setting up meetings and inviting the people I met.

One of the products we had was a water filtration system and I made that my flagship product. I decided to really get into water and focus on that product. It was the easiest thing to sell, too, because it really worked. All I had to do to sell it was get into a person's home. We had some simple tests we could run to show the potential customer the impurities in their tap water. Once we showed them the test results, we could run some of their water through our filtration system and show them the results again.

The tests made it pretty hard to walk away from the product. Who wants to be drinking all those chemicals? Bathing in them?

Washing their clothes or their children in them? The answer is nobody. So I'd lead with that product and secure the sale without too much difficulty. My tactic was to get in and show the test results, then let the person try the product for a few days. We had a great conversion rate on that product and my business started to grow — slowly at first, but then more and more quickly as we picked up team members. Obviously, when I went in to make a pitch I was hoping to recruit a new member of my business organization, but I was happy to just have a buying customer too.

Over the next five years I worked my MLM business basically full-time. I would do eight to twelve events a week in an effort to reach out and build the business. Part of my time was also tied up in recruiting and training my new team members. To accelerate the growth of the team, I put ads in the newspaper (something that worked back then but which I would never do today) and talk to everyone I met. I was dedicated and driven, and I was going to make a success out of the opportunity or die trying.

Expanding and Contracting

Early on in my time with that first networking company, unrelated to the business, my dad announced that he was taking the family to Disney World in Florida and asked if I wanted to go with them. I wasn't established yet, so I was still in "starving student" mode. I agreed to go only if I didn't have to pay my way because I couldn't yet afford it even if I'd wanted to. As it turns out, my dad's high school buddy lived down in Florida. They'd stayed in touch over the years and he'd agreed to let us all stay at his house.

We flew to Florida to stay for two weeks at their house. That was when I met his family and specifically, that's when I met his daughter. She was, ironically, going to school out in Idaho not far from where my family lived, but she was home on break for the first few days of our vacation. She left just a couple days after we arrived but I got to meet her just long enough to stir my interest. After Disney World, I looked her up, we dated for some time and eventually married. I don't think our dads ever dreamed that their children would end up married to each other. My father-in-law has joked that he would have moved farther away if he'd known his daughter was going to marry one of Vince's sons. All joking aside, God knew we would be right for each other and both of our fathers are exemplary men for our boys to follow. I am ever grateful for that fateful trip to Disney World.

While Keri and I were dating, and then after we were married, I was still working my networking business. I was doing everything I could to grow my team and increase my producer base. I was having some success by this time, but it was erratic, to say the least.

Having never been in network marketing before I was just doing what I'd been told. I'd been advised that having a training program was crucial, so I had one. I quickly learned that when I was enrolling people, the biggest question they had was "How do I sell this stuff?" Since then, I've learned that the "how" is less important than the "why." If people know the "why," they can figure out the "how" all on their own, but that's another story.

To answer that "how" question initially, I did a lot of training and a lot of my training was around the concept of landing a large first order. I was still new, so I was just teaching what I'd been taught. I didn't know that there was a better way. Thanks to my efforts and the efforts of my ever-expanding team, we soon had thousands of people involved and my income grew as my organization grew. I was finally having some success in the network marketing business but my income was hard to predict. I'd make $20,000 one month and then $5,000 the next, never knowing what the following month would bring.

I still made it work, however. I just had to work that much harder to find new people to bring into the team, new customers and business partners. The months where I was successful in finding new people meant I was successful in making money. If I didn't find as many new people, I didn't make as much.

During this time Keri and I moved to Scottsdale, Arizona to

live with my in-laws, who had recently relocated there from Florida. There's something about living with one's in-laws that everyone should have the opportunity to experience. You gain a much better appreciation for your spouse and where he or she came from. You also learn how to be ready for anything.

While we were living with my in-laws, my parents came down to visit. My wife was out with her sister, and my parents teamed up with her parents and sat me down in the living room for what I would now consider to be an intervention.

They proceeded to tell me that I was being irresponsible by pursuing a career in network marketing. They told me that I wasn't being a good husband or future father by being so reckless. Once they had established that I was delusional and irresponsible, they shifted gears and started telling me that I needed to give up network marketing and find a "real job," one with benefits and security. They went on for half an hour or so about how I needed to get my act together and give up the fantasy of network marketing. I know they only had our best interest at heart and I do not fault them in any way. The interesting thing was their timing. I wasn't yet "raking in the money," but Keri and I were starting to see some progress.

Keri proved to be invaluable during this process when she became aware of comments made during "the intervention". You see, coming from a home where her own parents were self-employed, she had learned to have gratitude for the God-given freedoms we enjoy. Knowing that we all have a stewardship to seek out, gain knowledge, and ask for Gods help to develop and flourish within that stewardship. She had learned to take to the Lord in prayer our questions about desired paths, and that after receiving answers, we move forward with all we have. Taking faithful steps into the unknown are all a part of my wife's history, an invaluable part, as she watched her own parents valiantly struggle and grow, win and lose in the world of business. We are accountable to God for how we move forward, and not just endure, but thrive in our ups and downs. She believed in me, and that we were doing what we were supposed to be

● ● ●

doing.

Our parents were right; stability is good, desirable, and necessary. Her parents knew the struggles and blessing of self-employment, my parents new the stability of a good job.

Part of the problem was that a lot was going on behind the scenes that our parents couldn't see. What they could see was the glitzy lifestyle that the company culture exuded. Keri never fell for that, she came from a solid hardworking, humble background. Muscles were built into her family but they came from work, sweat, and learning. Some in the company I worked with constantly touted "Fake it until you make it". That never sat well with us. Keri would retort "Faith it till you make it, for if you don't, then it was never real and fake is all a person turns out to be."

I'd been taught what to do to have success. I was following those steps and I was having success that our parents couldn't yet see. So I thanked them for their time and concern and went to the meeting I'd scheduled for that night and continued to do all the things I'd been taught. It was that simple. At least, it was that simple until we got a call one fateful morning. At this point, Keri and I had been married for a bit and we were finally starting to feel secure enough on this income rollercoaster that we could take the next step in our family life. We decided to have a baby.

The crucial call came shortly before Keri was due with our first little boy. The news was not good. My network marketing company no longer existed. Locks were on the doors of the main company for reasons that were never made clear to me. It was over, and there was no mistake about that. There would be no more product shipments, no new enrollments, and no more training. Everything was being liquidated for pennies on the dollar. We were done.

We later learned that the owner of the company had been foolish and had gotten caught up in the glitz and glamour of being at the top of a successful company and had brought the whole thing crashing down with his poor choices. Overnight, we went from

● ● ●

having a team of thousands and a pretty decent paycheck, to having nothing – no income and basically no team. And this was just as my first child was about to be born.

I sometimes hear people talk about network marketing as some sort of scam, where average people can't make a real go of it, or it's just a refuge for con artists. Unfortunately, that does apply to a miniscule number of people who choose to go into network marketing, as I suppose it applies to some people who go into police work, accounting, or construction. The few bad apples spoil it for everyone else who are trying to do things right and spread the success around. In reality it's not an accurate description of the vast majority of those in network marketing. We're not that different from the corner store that popped up down the street from you recently. We want to earn your business, as does the corner store. We just have a different, more effective method of distributing products and drumming up that business. Instead of sitting on the corner with a building full of product, we actually go out and prospect for customers to buy product directly from us. We believe in our product enough that we want to evangelize it. We want to tell people about it in a more effective way than just blasting the airwaves full of commercials to which no one pays attention. Still, the nature of networking is both good and bad in terms of a business model, and the success can easily go to a person's head if he's not a good person at the core, bringing the whole thing crashing down on everyone else's heads.

The Pyramid "Scheme"

The idea of being involved in a "pyramid" shaped distribution network never really bothered me. But having my business ignorantly labeled as a "scheme" in occasional conversations never felt particularly good, especially given that I was engaged in a legitimate business. If you have a $1 bill, pull it out and turn it over. If you don't have one on you, try to imagine one or do an Internet search for the back of the $1 bill. As you look at it you will see a pyramid on the left side. Do you know why? Because a pyramid is about the most stable structure that exists. Many of the Founding Fathers were Masons and they understood the innate strength of a pyramid, both symbolically and physically.

Do you know how many levels there are in the pyramid on the back of the dollar bill? Thirteen. There's one layer for each of the 13 colonies because the colonies were going to come together to support each other and a higher ideal. Notice also that the pyramid is unfinished, symbolizing room to grow, the ability of that pyramid to take on more weight and structure. The Founders used the pyramid symbol because they understood how strong the structure is and how it can stand the test of time.

That's why the great structures of Egypt were built as pyramids. The ancient Egyptians certainly had the architectural ability to create other, magnificent structures. We have so much of their culture preserved today in what they built thousands of years ago, but nothing has weathered time like those pyramids. The ancient American peoples built with pyramids too, and many of those pyramids stand today. Even mountains, in effect, are pyramids; they just happen to be pyramids with round bases built on huge scales. Still, they have a single point at the top — a summit — and sloping sides down to a wide base. The pyramid is inherently stable and long-lasting. What's more, every company and even the government are actually structured as a pyramid, though many refuse to acknowledge that idea. In a company, you have the executives at the top, some number of layers of management going down to the line workers who run the production. You could look at that as the base, but it's really not. You and I are the base of those pyramids. We're the consumers. We purchase the products and start the flow of money and power upward.

If everyone in the country suddenly, simultaneously stopped buying shampoo (or soda, cars, toilet paper, Styrofoam cups, etc.) the companies that sell shampoo and other consumables would quickly burn through all their reserve cash and go bankrupt. They rely on us, the base of the pyramid, to support the rest of the infrastructure.

And government is no different. "We the People" form the tax base from which all of government is funded — or should be funded. Whether you tax the rich or the middle class or everyone, those people form a pyramid. If they all suddenly left the country, the whole government infrastructure would collapse under its own weight. Sadly, if the government continues to grow at a faster rate than the base, it will eventually collapse in the same way for the same reason. The top of the pyramid should never outgrow the base. That's a fundamental law.

Violation of that law is the reason that in some places, network marketing has developed such a bad name over the years. People at the top have a huge pull on them to let their egos out, to swell up their pride and get greedy — as in almost all industries and pursuits. When that happens, the organization beneath can't grow quickly enough to support the imbalance at the top, and the whole structure collapses.

That's why Ponzi schemes, which are *NOT* network marketing organizations, are doomed to failure. Mathematically, the scheme itself will eventually require more people than there are in the world, and the whole thing will fall apart. Network marketing companies that focus on the compensation plan, rather than quality product, run that same risk. Any product distribution chain that focuses on profits rather than product runs that risk. Some of the network marketing companies of the 90s were built that way, and they collapsed, just like many other companies.

The fact of the matter is the network marketing of the 90s is dead. In the 90s — when I started — the profession was all about the compensation plans and fast talking. It was all about frontloading and closing the deal. It was all about the cars, the houses, the jewelry, the trips, the triple-diamond-presidential-grand-poobah-plenipotentiary-ruler-of-the-universe club, and all the other attendant benefits. It was all about being at the peak of the pyramid and not about cultivating a strong base.

That's gone today. I'll admit that I got sucked into it a little bit at the time, but Keri was a great grounding influence on me. As soon as my ego started to inflate a bit, she'd come running with a pin, or a hammer and nail, depending on what was needed to pop that balloon. No matter how hard I tried to get sucked into it, she would keep me out and help me keep my head and priorities straight.

Having that first network marketing company come crashing down was something of a wakeup call for me. It was a reminder that success can't be built in the clouds but must be cultivated on a principled foundation, grounded firmly until it grows to touch the clouds. You can't skip the foundational component. You have to grow the base before you can grow the peak.

A Team of One

When that first network marketing company came down, I lost most of my team. I'd built up a network of thousands of people and most of them left to find other work. I couldn't blame them. I didn't really have anything to offer at that point.

I didn't lose the whole team, however. Some of us were still sure that the solution for quality, residual income was in network marketing and we were ready to find a new opportunity and get on board with it. We understood that the company leadership may have been wrong but the concept was still right.

Our next attempt came in the form of a company that sold Website templates. This was around 1999 and the Internet was just taking off. Our premise was that you could make a lot of money by getting in on the Internet when it was just starting. In addition, my upline leader was so good, so dynamic in front of a room, that she could sell anything. The compensation structure at that new company looked promising so we joined on and started selling my upline leader. We weren't even selling a product anymore. These were my dark days in network marketing, but from this experience I learned to look for three product traits before investing my time and resources into a company. We'll cover those traits in just a bit.

● ● ●

After about three months my wife and I were looking for a new home again because the Website template company had failed to pay us for any of our work. We were fighting hard to maintain the team but people were dropping right and left to find other work because none of us could afford to be working for free. We settled on another little networking startup company and began gearing up our distribution organization yet again. This time, we chose a company with a tangible product that I felt had some real potential. It was a vitamin spray that met the three traits I had identified after the last failure, so we got everything in place and went to work.

Three months later, the company failed. Turns out, the leadership had no idea what they were doing and the company was under funded. It had ramped up too quickly, outstripped its supply chain, and grown itself to death – rookie mistake. Again, we didn't get paid.

At that point, we really only had one team member left: me. Keri and I were done with the MLM industry. We'd expended all our assets over the previous six months of not getting paid, and we had nothing left. We were so far under that we didn't even wait for the dealership to come and repossess our car, we took it to them. I didn't want the neighbors to see what we were going through as we filed for bankruptcy. We had to give up our house and move into a tiny, nasty basement apartment.

I can remember one evening when Keri hung up the phone and turned to me. It was just before our son was born, and she had tears in her eyes. She said, "Don't they know they can't get money out of a turnip?" We just didn't have anything left to give. If we'd had the money, we'd have paid our bills. We weren't, and aren't, the type to make an agreement and then walk away. This was the hardest time in my life. I had built a great business team and made all kinds of promises to people about how we were going to take care of each other, and now, for reasons beyond my control, those promises were breaking all around me. I couldn't keep the team together on broken promises, and everything fell apart very quickly.

At this point in my life I had a choice to make. I could continue to go straight down the path of probable destruction, or I could do something to stop the hemorrhaging and bring my family's financial situation back to health. During those years as a network marketer, I'd actually made a statement on stage that went something like, "I am permanently unemployable." The idea was that we had this big, great team, and I would never be able to find a job that took care of me and others the way that team had. I ate my words, tightened my belt, and went out to find a job.

In hindsight, I can see any number of things that I could have changed to prevent my family from suffering through this tragedy. I could have better scrutinized the Website template product and taken my team elsewhere. I could have looked at the management structure in the startup and taken my team elsewhere. I could have set aside more of my earnings and held more money in a "rainy day" fund. Truthfully, I wouldn't change anything. As awful as it was to go through at that time, I survived it. My family survived it. We made it through, and we learned and grew so much from those experiences. To change things would rob us of everything that we gained by being tempered in that fire of hardship.

If not for those experiences, how could I go to a person today and say to them, "I've been there. I've lost my house and car. There's a way out." If I hadn't been through those learning opportunities how could I mentor others through it? So, as painful as it was to go through that time in my life and take my lovely wife with me, I wouldn't change it. We learned and grew too much, and it taught me a stability and determination that has served me since. I know my limits better than most people, so I know just how far I can push to get results.

Finding the Essentials

For a short time after leaving the vitamin-spray startup, I got a job working in an anti-telemarketing firm. The founder absolutely hated telemarketers and was trying to develop a product that would make life miserable for them. It was really fun to be on the other side of the sales channel looking at ways to shut down direct sales, but I knew it wasn't a career for me. I took the job to put food on the table for my young family.

Thankfully, my background left me well positioned to take a job in network marketing again. The difference is that I wasn't going back into the distribution and sales side. I didn't have the financial wherewithal to make that journey from scratch again, now that my team had all gone their separate ways. The shift back into the distribution side would have to come later.

Instead, I got a job with an essential oils network marketing company on their corporate side. The woman who had been my old upline leader got me started there. She'd found a job with them as their marketing director and she recommended that I come in and interview. I did, and I got hired on to build a training program for them, which was something I'd done plenty in my previous opportunities. Interestingly, I'd actually been a distributor for the company for years, but I hadn't really involved myself with the business side of things because I liked the products and was just looking for the discount.

Although I had been introduced to and fallen in love with the product years before, they changed their business plan so frequently, their compensation structure was impossible to predict. So, instead, I just quietly ordered and used the products and didn't worry about the business.

Once I signed on as an employee my job was to develop a training program and implement it throughout the organization. It really wasn't any different than what I'd done before and what I've done since. And, it's what I enjoy, so it was a great fit.

Up to that point, there was no formal training mechanism in place for the company. When new distributors came on board, they were basically left to fend for themselves. Any training was informal and done purely on the distributor side, with upline leaders training their downlines. My goal was to create a series of trainings for the distributors, teaching people how to build a distributorship business, and another series for the product, teaching people about how to use the oils and what oils to use for what ailments. As it turned out, we trained mainly on the product, not the business.

I enjoyed the work, and I loved many of the people I worked with, but as time passed it became clear I wasn't really a good fit for the company culture. I didn't always see eye-to-eye with the executives and the decisions they made. I also ached to be back out in the field. When I had told distributors at events that I was permanently unemployable, I was being serious. I didn't like the corporate life that revolved around showing up at a set time and leaving at a set time, putting in the "seat miles" in between.

I wanted the freedom to go and do and be rewarded for my intelligence and effort, not for my time. So a few years in, I started looking around for an established distributorship that I could buy. I didn't have any luck. Funny thing about network marketing is that the successful people don't generally want to give it up once they get going, and the unsuccessful people don't stay in it long enough to create a business worth buying. Keri and I had actually been running several small side businesses, our goals were set, but we were not satisfied.

So I kept looking, without success, for several years. I actually found several perfect spots but I couldn't get anyone to bite on selling to me. I could have gone and started from scratch, but I had already built several businesses that way and lost them due to company problems. I didn't want to start over again, although this seemed like a solid company. Not to mention that after three or four years on the corporate payroll, my family was used to a certain level of income again — steady, predictable income. To start from scratch would have meant giving up that income again, and I wasn't quite ready to do that.

Then one day I was playing basketball with some guys from my church, and I'd brought my oldest son along. He was sitting on the sidelines and watching us while I ran up and down the court.

I don't even remember how I got roped into playing in the first place. Because basketball isn't really my sport, I wasn't really into the game. I was just kind of trotting back and forth and taking a few shots when I got the chance. Halfway through the game, my son finally yelled at me, **"Come on, Dad. Get off the bench, and get in the game!"**

I stopped right there in the middle of the court and turned to look at him. He was talking about the actual game of basketball that I was engaged in at the moment, but I heard his words in a whole different way. I realized that I wasn't really in the game of life anymore. This was true of my career and my life. I'd taken the corporate job, and it had served a valuable purpose, but that purpose was served, and the need had passed. I had moved beyond it, and now I was just leaning on my job as a crutch. I knew that I wasn't a good fit for corporate life. That's not where my passion lies. I loved training, but I knew I could be a much more effective trainer if I were free to do it on my own terms, and was doing it to build my own business and future. We wanted out of where I was, for reasons beyond our own entrepreneurial spirits.

My son woke me up to my reality that day and I decided it was time to get serious about making a change. I wasn't just going to shop around for a distributorship that someone else was willing to sell; I was going to start actively looking for the next step in my career, my next adventure.

Leap of Faith

Around that time, in early 2008, I started to hear some rumors about a new startup company. I knew most of its principals from my associations within the field of network marketing and some from my time at the job I had at the time. Some of them had also tried out the corporate side for a time before moving on, and I had gotten to know them during their tenure.

At that time I'd been at my corporate position for about seven years and I really did want to get back out in the field. When my son told me to get off the bench and get back in the game, it just hammered home that need in my mind. I couldn't deny it anymore, so I started doing some asking around. I started trying to find out more about this new startup and what kind of an opportunity it might be.

The problem was that I couldn't get any details from anyone. No one who actually knew anything would tell me anything about it, because some of the principals had come from my employer and I was still there. Those principals had signed non-solicit contracts when they left, contracts that prevented them from coming back and trying to headhunt at my company, and these people were true to their word. They had integrity. That meant that they couldn't tell me anything about what they were doing. So the only bits and pieces of information I could get came to me circuitously, as rumors and possibilities. None of it was straight from the source, and I had no way of knowing whether or not any of it was true.

I actually ran into one of the prospective founders at the store one Saturday and thought to myself, *here's my chance. I'm finally going to get some answers.* This particular founder had been a close colleague for a number of years. We had traveled and trained together extensively. I thought that if anyone was going to tell me anything, it would be him. When I saw him at the store that day, by total coincidence, I knew I had to make my move. I had to find out more.

I went over to him and said, "Okay. What are you doing? Because I'm hearing all this stuff, so just tell me what you're doing."

He looked at me and smiled and said, "Oh. Hi Justin. How's your wife doing?"

I wasn't going to have any of that. I wasn't going to let him get off so easily. So I continued, "No, no, no. That wasn't the question. Let me rephrase the question: Tell me that you're *not* starting a company."

He dodged again. "So, how are the kids?"

But now I had him. "Okay. If you *weren't* starting a

• • •

27

company, you'd just tell me that you weren't. But, since you won't say that you aren't, and you won't say that you are, it means that you are; you just can't talk about it with me."

That gave me at least one essential answer without him actually saying anything to me. I could safely surmise that he was indeed starting a company. There wasn't a way to back him into a corner on how the business was going to be structured or what they would be selling or any of the other details, but at least I knew there was a company being started.

I knew this meant there was a chance to get back in the game. Unfortunately, it also would require a leap of faith on my part, and on the part of my family. We couldn't get any of the details about the company, so if we were going to join up, we were going to just have to step out into the darkness and hope that there was something there. That meant walking away from a pretty decent salary, benefits, and great bonuses. It was not an easy step for me to take, but Keri was ready. Because of her childhood, she knew the hardships that came with owning your own business. She also knew one very important fact. I would be happier chasing my dreams than building someone else's. She encouraged me to quit my job and said, "We will live on rice and beans until you find what makes you happy."

I walked away from my corporate career and went to talk to that same principal and the other owners about their new venture. They could talk to me now because I had severed my ties with my employer. That's when I found that the new company wasn't actually ready yet. Nobody was going to be paid for at least six months, possibly more. Even with this reality, that first night Keri said to me, "Don't walk back, run back!"

The thought of not having an income for a number of months was unnerving, however, the opportunity and potential were both there; they were just a bit further out on the time horizon than originally anticipated. At this point, we had some savings and a 401(k), so we didn't walk from everything straight into nothing exactly; it just meant we were going to have to live very frugally for a while.

Laying the Groundwork

When I signed on with this new venture, I was signing on to a dream. Really, that's all it was. The original five founders had come together to share a common dream about a company and a proposed line of products, but nothing had really come together yet. We didn't have any sales materials, Websites, brochures, or product samples. In fact, we didn't actually even have any product yet.

We didn't even have a name. We called ourselves "NewCo", which was short for "New Company" because we didn't yet know what we were going to name ourselves. With all that nothing in hand, we hit the road to talk about what was coming, even though we didn't have anything tangible coming yet. All we had was a vision and faith….

…And one box of sample product. We had one box of selected essential oils and they were light-years beyond the quality of anything I had experienced up to that point in my life. I'd thought I'd known essential oils from my prior experiences but this was a whole new level of potency and quality.

The problem was that we only had that one box, which meant we couldn't give out any product samples, and we had to be very careful about what happened to the box. We would pass it around at events so that potential customers and distributors could smell the product, but we had to watch the box like hawks to make sure everything came back. We couldn't even let people use the oils yet, because everything would have been used up in very little time. We couldn't afford to lose any of the samples because at that point, they were irreplaceable.

I actually have people who come up to me today and tell me how they wish they had known about dōTERRA (we finally did name the company) in the beginning. They wish they could have gotten involved right at the start. My answer to them is "you are." We're only six years in, and things are still at the beginning stages.

My other answer to them is "be glad you're involved now and not back then." Now we have Websites, support materials and product samples — and product. Even when we first started getting product in, there was a lot of room for improvement. Initially, our labels washed off. The glue for the labels was water-based, and it would come apart if it got wet or even too humid. It was always fun trying to guess which oil you had after the label came off. That's no longer an issue. That problem, and a host of others, has been solved. But to solve those problems, we had to go through that process. Someone had to cross all those rivers and build all the bridges. Someone had to fail the trials and make the errors so that we'd know where and how to improve. Anyone joining today has the advantage of almost seven years of learning and experience to build on. We had none of that initially.

Being the Beginning

When people come up to me and tell me they wish they'd been there in the beginning, they're really saying they wish the tree had grown up all around them so that they can sit on their hands and make money without any effort. It doesn't work that way. If you don't work, you won't be a top Wellness Advocate, which is what we call our distributors. If you do work, you can be the top Wellness Advocate regardless of when you joined.

I, like many others, earned my position by putting in all that time and effort for no pay at the start of the company. We earned our positions by selling people on an idea with no name and a box of sample oils. We put in all kinds of effort and time, and built a great business, yet even I, who was there from the very beginning, have to continue to work at my business every day or it will go stagnant and disappear over time. No one gets a free lunch. Business doesn't work that way.

That first box of product samples I mentioned earlier, in fact, was critical for us. When I signed on to a new, nameless startup, the thing that kept me on for all those paycheck-less months was that box of product samples. I knew what was coming, and I knew it was amazing. We didn't have anything else ready yet, but at least I could get the vision of what was going to be.

I had been working at the other company for years, and I thought I knew what quality essential oils were. When I was introduced to the oils that dōTERRA was going to sell, I couldn't deny the difference. In fact, one of the things they did to confirm my enthusiasm for the new path I had chosen was to pass me a bottle of my favorite oil. They passed me that bottle, I took a sniff, and I was all in. I soon discovered that there was a whole world of essential oil manufacturers out there that my former company didn't have relationships with. Some of them were cheap, discount producers and made products unworthy of buying, but a few made the very highest quality products. Those were the producers dōTERRA went to for our products, and the difference was obvious.

The product was the big sales point for me. Once I smelled that quality difference, I couldn't go back. Additionally, I didn't want to go back to the management team and structure I'd left behind. I'd had my run-ins with them, and we'd frequently had differences of opinion.

I knew most of the owners of dōTERRA because I'd worked with them before in various capacities. I knew their character and integrity, and I knew their style of management and their vision. I knew that I would be so much happier working with them than I ever could have been with the steady paycheck and great bonuses I was leaving behind. So I was totally sold on dōTERRA even before it had a name.

Having the best quality product, however, means nothing when you haven't started getting the product in to ship yet. Having great leadership doesn't mean anything when they have no money to pay anyone yet. That first year, while we were getting everything set up, was extremely uncertain for everyone. The owners had planned for a long burn time before the revenue started, but that didn't make it any easier on them to see the money going out when nothing was coming back in.

Keri had immersed herself in financial education, reading a number of books after our earlier financial fall – books to teach her how to better manage our household. We'd been through the dark days of collection and bankruptcy, and we weren't anxious to go back. It was humiliating and difficult enough the first time around. We'd fully climbed out of that hole during our corporate job time, and Keri was determined to not let us fall down there again. Her motto, which became useful in creating stability for our family became, "Sacrifice now to have more later." I was also determined to make sure that it never happened again. In fact, that's one of the things that drove us to work so hard to get dōTERRA up and running.

Becoming dōTERRA

It's important to explain how the owners of the new company we were building put everything on the line for dōTERRA, including their homes, their life-savings, and all of their combined financial resources. Most of them did not take a salary for the first year or more. Any of us that were there in that startup phase sacrificed all financial stability to help get the ball rolling. We were fortunate enough to begin the company with a small group of team members who were passionate about our product and had really captured the vision of where the company could go. Truly, the credit for our success belongs to these amazing, passionate and determined leaders who were willing to put it all on the line and work hard when we had little more than a vision of where we wanted to go.

For the first three years of my association with dōTERRA, I was still driving my 1997 Honda Civic – the basic transportation that had faithfully carried me back and forth to my office cubicle for years. It was red except for a different shade of red on the trunk and front bumper. By three years in, the business had grown, the product was available, and we were making money. We were, in fact, making enough money that we could have bought a new Honda Civic every month, but I was still driving that beater from the late 90s.

Why?

Because it got great gas mileage, it ran well, and it was paid for. My wife's financial discipline and our determination to live well within our means had taught me that there was no reason to go spending money to replace something that wasn't broken. I didn't need a new car when the one I had worked just fine. My ego didn't demand that I be seen driving around in a fancy car. That all changed when I realized that my car was actually hurting my business.

I pulled up in front of the building one day just as a group of partners from Asia were out taking a smoke break. They all saw me and started talking. I couldn't understand what they were saying, but I could understand their looks well enough and I knew that they knew approximately how much money I was making. They knew my level in the company, yet here I was driving this old beater of a car. The story didn't match between what they were being told regarding the possibilities with dōTERRA and what they were seeing in terms of my outward show of success. I realized that the inconsistency could drive away potential business and that was when I decided I needed to get something new.

Many of my financial decisions have been made that way since our financial fall. Before that failure I got sucked in (to an extent) to the multi-level marketing culture of big trips, big houses, and new cars. Keri did a great job of keeping me grounded, but I still got sucked in a little. After those dark days between companies, we decided to keep our heads on straight and not fall for the hype anymore.

In many instances, dōTERRA operates in the same way in terms of finances and decision- making. Decisions aren't reached in terms of what will best help the Triple-Diamond President's Club and the company's owners. Decisions are made to best help the product, the company as a whole, and the base of the distribution organization. Rather than focusing at the top and potentially unbalancing things, focus is directed at the base, where the business

• • •

ballast is, to strengthen the core of the business. We focus on the benefits of our product and not our compensation structure. In that regard, we're kind of the opposite of many of the other companies I had worked with, and we're better off for it. We're also kind of the opposite of that vitamin-spray start-up company, in that dōTERRA rapidly became cash flow positive and debt- free. We didn't start that way, but we made decisions to pay off debt and secure the business rather than bonusing everyone with fancy trips and other bells and whistles.

Still, in the beginning days of the company, things were difficult and tight. We were traveling and laying the groundwork for what was to come, and that required investment, although nothing was coming in just yet. We had to pay for the business long before the business began to pay anything back.

And that's how business goes. You must put the effort and capital in before you can pull anything out. People often fail to recognize that connection, and they often fail because of it. In a relationship, you call it "sacrifice." You sacrifice your time, effort and attention in order to curry favor with someone else, whether it's a friend, family member, significant other, or spouse. You give up something now in order to secure something even better down the road, and the moment you stop giving to the relationship, it starts to fall apart. That degradation may start slowly, and take a long time, but it starts immediately, make no mistake.

Business works the same way. You have to sacrifice. You have to give up time, effort, and money now in order to secure dividends down the road. And just like a relationship with another person, if you stop investing — stop sacrificing — the business will immediately start failing. We were all on board with dōTERRA, we wanted to see the company succeed, and we were willing to give our time and effort without pay to see it through. It was hard, but it was worth it for what we have now created.

Ultimately, we decided on the Latin name, dōTERRA as the name for our company, which means "gift of" (dō) "the earth" (terra). Incidentally, it's pronounced with a long-O sound: dō, as in "no" not do, as in "dew." Some people disagree on that point because they like the action implicit in the verb "to do," but that doesn't change the correct pronunciation or the history behind the concept of a gift from the earth.

Once we had a name, we could start looking into things like Websites and support materials. Then we started to get product in and we started to sell our products and change lives. Since that time business has taken off. We're still in the beginning stages, in my mind, but the company has grown enough and made enough to pay off its start-up debts and establish itself as a stable, lasting company. Because of an amazing team we're enrolling more than 50,000 people in our business organization every month and have more than a million members worldwide. It's just a drop in the bucket compared to the company's potential but it's a good start. Our mission to heal the world, physically and financially has never been more secure.

About This Book

So that's the introduction to this amazing profession of network marketing. If that's all you're reading it for, we're done. Congratulations!

If you're reading for tips on how to "get rich quick" in the world of network marketing, you're also done. There will be no such tips in this book because they don't exist. This is the wrong business for that kind of mindset. I will be sharing with you the principles and concepts that helped me and my associates establish an enduring enterprise worth millions of dollars, but I won't lie to you and tell you that it was quick or easy. In fact, I'll warn you it was just the opposite.

You've already read about the time we spent, without a paycheck, to lay the foundations for the success we're enjoying at dōTERRA today. Even now, however, we haven't "made it," as some might think. We still go out and make our contacts. We still recruit new team members and customers. We still invest in our business.

In short, we still hold fast to the principles I'm going to teach you about in this book. Why? Because I still want to be successful, and, the moment I turn off these principles, I will turn off their power and my success will dry up.

I have written this book to be the compilation of every training or seminar I have ever given on this business. I may not have space to fit in all the awkward moments and truth-is-stranger-than-fiction stories, but I'll do what I can. I'll also make sure that all the principles are included.

By reading this book you will have the information necessary to go out and build a successful dōTERRA business. You'll have everything you need to build the life you desire. But I won't tell you that it's easy. It's not. It requires dedication and patience. It requires perseverance and discipline. It requires a deeper resolve than just a desire to make money. That won't cut it on the hard days, and there will be hard days. Plenty of them.

• • •

If you want to make the most of these principles, you'll need to dig deeper than just wanting a paycheck, because you can go anywhere to get a paycheck. You'll need to have reasons strong enough to motivate you when nothing seems to be going right because there will be days when nothing seems to go right.

That said, the concepts are straightforward, and anyone can have success in abundance by following them. In fact, I know of a couple in New Mexico who have used these principles to become one of the top-producing couples at dōTERRA. They make more in a month now than they did in a year before, and these people are not Ivy League grads with silver spoons. They are simple, ordinary, everyday folks, like anyone else out there. The thing that really makes them special is their drive, their "why." It motivates them to do more and to stick it out when times get tough.

Network marketing is an amazing profession, so don't let me dissuade you from the path by confirming the realities of hard work. The success, physically and financially, are there for the taking. You just need to be diligent. These principles work, and they're simple, but that doesn't mean they're easy. In fact, that difference is probably as good a place as any to start.

1. Simplicity

"Everything should be made as simple as possible, but not simpler." — *Einstein*

The first thing you need to know is that nothing I'm going to present to you in this book is complicated. Some of the concepts will require more practice and thought than others, but there's no fancy algorithm in these pages that only that engineer up the street from you can understand. I won't try to wow you with concepts too convoluted for the average person, and I won't tell you that I have the magic box that no one can understand but from which everyone can benefit. I'm not going to tell you to "just trust me and do this." Let's just lay everything out for you in detail so that you can make an educated decision to follow the advice, or not. Either way, the choice will be yours and it will be based on understanding.

This process will give you the opportunity to grow but we'll do it in a way that you can understand what you're getting into. Having the blind lead the blind is a bad idea, so I'll do everything possible to remove the blindfold and pull these principles out of their block boxes. We'll put everything on display here.

We'll do this for two reasons: First, there's nothing to hide. I can point to any number of people who have learned these concepts, applied them, and are now enjoying fabulous success. There's no need to hide the recipe for the secret sauce because there's nothing in it that would embarrass me or anyone else or that would detract from my own opportunities or success. Quite the opposite. I'm not trying to trick anyone into giving me anything. I want to help people find their own success because it's only as others enjoy success that I am successful.

Second, let's focus on your experiences and knowledge. Let's help you find success and growth. Experience tells us that we can have far more success helping others find their own success than by jealously hoarding principles and wresting success out of the hands of others. We grow more quickly when others around us are growing

• • •

too. That's the "networking" part of our business. The anonymous quote, "A rising tide lifts all boats" holds true here. So does the John Donne quote, "No man is an island, entire of itself." It's as true of business as it is of life — we all depend on others to help us succeed.

We already enjoy a degree of success. What good does it do to carve out more for ourselves? The next level of success for us is to lift others and hopefully watch them sail past us.

Simple vs. Easy

That said, let me clarify something. When most people hear the word "simple" they usually misconstrue the meaning to be "easy." On the one hand, that's correct. Simple things have a certain predisposition toward being easy as well. They are easy to understand, and it's usually easy to see the application. Once you have those points out of the way it should be pretty easy to put the principle to work in your life, right?

Actually, falling into the trap of equating "simple" and "easy" is a surefire way to cause yourself headache and heartache down the road. The reason is that simple things usually *are* easy to do. However, because they are simple, they are also easy to *not* do. That's just a fact of life. It's a simple thing to see a penny on the ground, bend down, and pick it up. There's nothing complicated about that string of events. It's even easy to do. But how often do we do it? Instead, we rationalize that a penny is virtually worthless, and we keep walking. What if that were a $100 bill on the ground. Would you stop and pick it up then? Why? Because the $100 bill has more value than the penny? Isn't money just money, regardless of the denomination? And isn't free money free, again, regardless of the denomination?

In any case, the principles for success in the networking profession are simple. For example, "Make two new contacts and two follow-up contacts per day" is simple. Do you agree? In fact, it's simple almost to the point of being childish. What if in an eight-hour work day you took two hours for each contact? Is that simple?

Yes, but it requires your time and effort, consistently and relentlessly. Yet it's a powerful principle that will yield wild amounts of success over the span of a career.

How complicated is it to pick up the phone and make two phone calls? Or turn around and talk to the person behind you in line at the grocery store? Strike up a conversation with the person on the next bike machine over at the gym? It's not complicated, it's simple. There is no need for Herculean strength or rocket-scientist intellect. Having a conversation doesn't require 12 years of medical school or other specialized or highly focused training. You don't need a license or certification to talk to another person.

But that doesn't mean it's easy. Believe it or not, the key difference between "simple" and "easy" is just paper. That's right. Paper.

On paper, anything simple looks easy. You can read through it and say to yourself "Yeah, I thought of that a long time ago." You don't need precise schematics or detailed processes for simple concepts. You just read them and understand them. Simple. Easy.

The difficulty arises when you put that simple act into practice. If you're not an outgoing person, turning around to chat with the person behind you at the store is anything *but* easy. Still simple, but far from easy. The same goes for making a couple of phone calls or sending a follow-up email or letter. Don't make it harder than it really is. Many have no problem talking to people, and this will be easy for them. I'm just acknowledging that not everyone finds this simple thing to be extremely easy.

It's also simple to book a conference room at your local library or call a friend to host a product class, but that doesn't mean it's easy. It's as simple as picking up the phone, dialing a number, and talking. Most of us do those things every day — sometimes without even thinking about them. But that doesn't mean it's easy to talk to a stranger or risk imposing on a friend. Even if your friend says yes, it's certainly not so easy to then go around inviting other people to show up to the class.

• • •

I told you about how my first class went. Even my own parents didn't show up. It was simple enough to put the presentation together; it was simple to find a venue; it was even simple to invite people to attend; and it would have been *easy* to quit right after that in-my-face failure. After all, not a single person showed up! I did all the simple things and nothing happened.

But that's where the difference between simple and easy really comes to light. It was simple to put all of those pieces together in order to host that class. It was equally simple to put all those pieces together to hold my second class; however, it was not easy either time. I was nervous enough the first time around, and the second time around was just bad. After such a blatant failure for the first event, it was anything but easy to put all that effort out again for the second event, but it was still simple.

Simple, then, refers only to the complexity of the task. Let's look at an example:

I'm a rocket scientist. It's true. I am, and you can be too. Here's how:

Get a two-liter soda bottle.

Clean out the bottle. This step is actually optional.

Get a rubber stopper with a hole in the center and insert the valve from a bike tire through the stopper. Make sure the valve is a tight fit. You can add a little epoxy to secure the valve if you're worried.

Fill the bottle about halfway with water and insert the stopper.

Attach a tire pump to the valve in the stopper, and set the rocket into launch position (with the valve pointed down and the bottom of the bottle pointed up). Your launch pad can be as sophisticated or simple as you'd like. A stack of books or a fallen log will do. Just make sure you use books you don't want anymore (because they will get really wet).

Pump the tire pump as hard and fast as you can.

If you were following along, you noticed that as you first

started pumping, nothing happened. Then, suddenly, the bottle blasted into the air along whatever trajectory angle you set, spraying water everywhere as it went.

Congratulations. You're a rocket scientist. It was that simple.

Still not convinced? That's because you understand that a "real" rocket — like NASA uses — is far more complex and involves chemicals and tolerances that would require specialized tools, materials, and education, which I don't have.

Still, we just built a real rocket which blasted off based on the same principles by which a NASA rocket blasts off. In fact, you can find instructions for building soda-bottle rockets on NASA's own Website. That makes us rocket scientists on a much simpler scale than the NASA approach.

Principles— *true* principles — are simple. If they weren't, nobody would be able to verify whether the concepts actually worked, or whether they were even actual principles. Just being simple, however, doesn't make them easy. And, easy or not, the simplicity of a principle doesn't make us immediately believe it. In fact, the opposite is often the case.

Complexity Crisis

In life, we are surrounded by simplicity, but we often refuse to accept it. The simple answer to financial problems is to spend less than you make. The solution to a healthy relationship is to do more good than harm to the person we say we love. These principles are so painfully simple and obvious, but most people walk right by them without a thought.

Why?

For some reason, simple has become a synonym for unintelligent. Rather than celebrating simplicity for its easily understandable and executable nature, we turn our backs on it. Instead, we equate credibility with complexity, correctness with sophistication. The harder it is to understand something the truer it must be, right? Sounds to me like we're suffering from a complexity crisis.

Perhaps this stems from how we've enshrined the sciences. Einstein, a certifiable genius, gave us "laws" like the Theory of Relativity and we accept it as gospel. What's interesting is the name of that discovery: the special THEORY of relativity. Einstein didn't claim that it was true. He didn't say it was flawless or perfect. He just said it was our best shot to date at explaining why certain complex things in physics happen the way they do — especially relating to light.

I don't wish to detract from the sciences here, but we tend to assume that scientists are right because we "mere mortals" have trouble understanding the Theory of Relativity (or any number of other scientific theories), while scientists (i.e., *smart* people) seem to have no trouble comprehending them. After all, they've spent a lot of time studying it all; shouldn't they have figured it out by now? Can't we just trust them to be right? Why should we need to understand it for ourselves?

This association between complexity and perceived correctness leads to a situation where we assume things are right when we can't quite understand them, as long as someone intelligent (an authority figure) tells us that the theory is sound. Basically, we accept for fact the things that someone else is paid to tell us in as confusing a way as possible. Don't laugh, it's true! If scientists were all after "the truth, the whole truth, and nothing but the truth," we wouldn't have so many instances where they form opposing camps over a topic — like global warming or string theory. Putting it that way, you can see how dangerous of a paradigm we've fallen into.

Most scientific "truths" are just theories, not rules or laws. They're mostly right — and usually "right enough" for people like you and me — but such complex ideas can't be effectively tested by us, so they can't be effectively proven or disproved in our minds. Scientists just test what they can, accept the rest, tentatively, and move on until something better comes along. Go look at the progression of our understanding of the solar system for an example. Does anyone still believe the earth is the center of the universe?

It's a fact that the Scientific Method of analysis taught in grade schools everywhere is actually incapable, by definition, of proving anything to be true. It's not built that way. The scientific method tells you to make a guess and then try to prove your guess wrong. If you're successful, you know your guess was wrong. If you're unsuccessful, you know only that your guess wasn't wrong this time. "Wasn't wrong this time" is not the same as "right," but we often, wrongfully accept it as truth.

This tendency toward putting a stamp of approval on anything we don't quite understand has led countless numbers of people in the opposite direction from success over the years. In the end, we don't value simple principles the way we should.

Simplicity Within

There is a reason that our challenges in life never seem simple or straightforward.

Why? Why can't it just be simple?

Well, the truth is that it can. The truth is also that emotions make things more complex than we'd care to admit. We're not aliens from a nearby planet who can simply ignore our emotions. Those emotions generate significant complexity in life. Add to that the fact that we grow up dealing with these messy, emotional, complex situations on a frequent basis and we all kind of end up expecting some complexity.

We've built entire industries around helping people delve into the complexity of emotion, and we've arrived at a point where we accept complexity as a part of life — even when it doesn't need to be. We've even gone so far as to enthrone as "gurus" the people who can see through the complexity.

It's really easy to understand simple principles. Because it's easy to understand them it's also easy to apply them. However, because it's easy to understand them, it's also easy to ignore or dismiss them. After all, life's problems feel so complex and heavy how could a simple solution ever be enough to solve them?

Can I tell you a secret now? The true gurus are those who "see through" the complexity and ignore it. They are looking through to the simplicity that underlies everything. They are looking to the simple roots that run beneath all the complication that we pile over the top.

That clarity of vision enables them to work with those simple, fundamental principles which have the most impact in life, business, relationships, and everywhere in between. They aren't necessarily any better at sorting out the chaos; they're just better at accepting that simple solutions really can be enough to solve complex problems.

Now, for a history lesson: During the Revolutionary War one of the reasons the Americans were able to hold their own against the British is because the Americans rarely met the British in a fair fight. The "rules of warfare" at the time indicated that you could only shoot the soldiers, not their leaders. Commanders were to be respected and treated as nobility (and many of them were).

The Americans came on the scene, desperately outmatched, and threw that convention out the window. They knew they couldn't win by dealing with the individual symptoms of the real threat. So, in many cases, rather than deal with the complexity of trying to shoot only the soldiers, the Americans would just shoot the British commanders. Without leadership the British didn't know what to do and the problem was quickly resolved. As morbid as it may seem, the American solution was a very simple one: cut off the head and the body dies. Go to the root cause and resolve it; the rest of the problem will work itself out. It's simple, but it works.

Of course, it's much easier to just deal with the symptoms in many cases. That's why so many people turn to medication to ease their pains when a simple exercise program would enable their bodies to better regulate and resolve their problems without medication. We're hardwired to believe that complexity is king. And it doesn't help that no matter how easy it might be to do something simple it's just as easy (if not easier) to do something else, often something more complex, to put blind faith in the unknown and hope for the best.

To Not To

Do you have children around who watch their favorite movies over and over? There's a Disney/Pixar movie my wife and children have seen many times called "Cars" in which cars take on human characteristics and live life like a human. In the movie, the main character, a hotrod race car named Lightning McQueen, ends up impounded in a backwater town far off the beaten track. The resident tow truck, Mater, is talking to Lightning when the local sheriff arrives and asks Mater a simple question:

"What did I tell you about talking to the accused?"

Mater, somewhat downcast, replies, "To not to."

A simple question is asked and a simple answer is given.

We all laugh at Mater's response. How easy would it have been for him to just drive by and never stop to chat? It would have been so easy "to not to."

The sneaky truth lurking behind Mater's response, however, has a far more profound impact than you'd expect from a movie for children. Because the truth is that it's so easy "to not to" when it comes to doing something…anything, whether that thing is good or bad.

It's easy to not exceed the speed limit. It's easy to not make a few phone calls today. It's easy to not write down that expense and count it against the budget. It's really easy to not follow your exercise program. It's easy to not read that self-improvement book you bought three months ago.

It's especially easy to not repeatedly do the simple things when our first efforts don't seem to achieve the desired results. The problem here is that we're looking for the atom bomb approach, the instant win, the "do this one thing and the whole world will bow at your feet" magic bullet by which we vaporize all our challenges.

• • •

Society has been trained to believe that bigger is better, that the next big thing is just around the corner, that big rewards require big risks. We want to be able to pull out the magic bullet, blast the competition/problem/heartache to smithereens and then roll in with our tanks as victorious, conquering heroes!

Doing something simple day in and day out just isn't impressive. It's boring and dull and *anything but* heroic. In reality, the solution isn't some big, complex, atom-bomb approach. There is no "get rich quick" solution — not a legitimate, legal, lasting one anyway. The answer for having amazing success in the networking profession is the simple approach; it's the steady repetition of a few simple yet key ideas that yield results over time.

I'm not here to tell you that this is the easy approach, however. If the networking profession were that easy, everyone would do it. They'd do it for the same reason that so many people actually *don't* do it: it would be the path of least resistance.

It's just too easy to *not* do these simple things. It's too easy to say to us, "I made my two contacts yesterday. I'll make my two contacts tomorrow. Today's just not a good day for me. I'm going to take a pass and not do it."

At the moment that someone asks themselves the question, "Am I going to make my contacts today?" more often than not the answer is along the lines of "Eh. Tomorrow." A grunt and a word. That's simple too, and it's easy.

The truly sad part is that you can get away with it for a while. Skipping a day won't kill you or sink your business but it will make it that much easier to skip the simple things the next time around, and the next. Pretty soon, you'll be skipping more days than you aren't — taking the "easy" path and then running to catch up because your business will be collapsing around you.

It's easy to do the simple things one time but it's also easy to *not* do them. It gets hard when you have to do those simple things over and over, day in and day out, without experiencing some atom-bomb success in the first two weeks. Every day it gets a little easier to stay on track and keep doing those simple things, but every day it gets easier to justify taking a day off, too. The option that you choose will ultimately make or break your success.

So keep in mind that nothing here will be complex or even novel in the sense of being some new, abstract, trendy process or method. What I'm going to teach you will be simple and straightforward, and it'll be up to you to either choose the easy path and maintain your current status quo or to embrace the simplicity, cut through the complexity, and find your success.

2. Three Essential Traits

"Courage is never to let your actions be influenced by your fears." — *Arthur Koestler*

The skills and talents necessary to have success in the networking profession are varied and numerous, but they actually aren't the most important part of finding success in the field. You can be the best presenter in the world and still fail. Conversely, you can be the worst presenter in the world and still have amazing success. I know people like that. Why is that the case?

Because someone out there will have the skill you need and you can always partner with that person to fill the gap in your own skill set. If you aren't good at something I suggest going forward anyway and start working on it. At the same time, don't stress about it too much. There's no reason to get bent out of shape over any of these skills or talents. If you'll take your courage in hand and choose the hard path by consistently doing the simple things, you will succeed. And, at some future date, you'll probably look back and see that you've developed a number of the skills in the process. Either way, until you develop the skills personally, you should look for mentors and examples to help you out. Don't have presentation skills? Find someone who does and bring that person in to do the presentation. It's that simple.

In fact, the networking profession is so simple, that you can actually have success without any natural skill or talent. That seems a bit farfetched, but it's true. You don't necessarily need to start with any skills or ability. You just need to have the courage to start. Be genuine and passionate and people will be interested in what you have to offer even if you don't offer all the answers. However, remember that anyone can be successful without the knowledge and talent, but that success will be limited in scope. Heightened levels of success require more and more from you, and you'll fail if you don't keep up.

● ● ●

As you start out, one of the keys to remember is that you can have success regardless of your skill level because you aren't the only variable involved. There's more to the equation than just you and the customer; there's also a product. If you pick the right product, it will basically sell itself and you can get by with being friendly and honest. But you can't just pick the perfect product and then be complacent. Eventually, the marketplace will defeat you if you try that tactic. Maintaining customers is easy if your product is the best of the best. But that initial purchase decision will be largely based on a potential customer getting to know *you*, liking you and believing that they can trust you.

For that reason, don't take this chapter as the solution to all your problems. I want to get you started, and I want you to understand the importance of the product, but I don't want to downplay the importance you have as the messenger. You need to be focused on self-improvement or you'll cap out your progress early on and start backsliding.

If you want to have a successful product in the business of network marketing, it needs to be three things:

1. It needs to be unique. You need to have a product nobody else has.
2. It needs to be one that people will want once they're educated about it.
3. It needs to be a consumable. Reordering is essential.

At dōTERRA, of course, our product fits all three of those criteria. That's one of the reasons we're growing so quickly — and one of the reasons why it's so easy to sell our oils. Still, to make sure you understand how these different traits interplay with your talents and skills, let's take a moment to review them in a bit more detail.

Unique

Network marketing is, at a very basic level, sales. The goal of building a team, making contacts (and everything else that we're discussing) is to sell product. That's where the revenue comes from. It may not require the tactics and gimmicks of the people down at the local used-car lot, but the networking profession is still a sales profession.

One of the problems people run into in sales is that of competition. Have you ever wondered why companies advertise? Because of their competition. When you go to the store are you going to buy Dole or Chiquita? Banquet or Green Giant? Are you going to shop at Wal-Mart or Costco (or somewhere else)? Do you want Michelin tires or Bridgestone? Will you fly Delta, Southwest, or United? We're surrounded by a mountain of products and hoards of service-providers, all clamoring for our attention and ultimately, our dollars. It's like being at a music festival. Rows of booths are set up and each booth houses a different band each one playing for all its worth in an effort to get an audience. Do you really want to set up in the next booth and play to the same crowd? Wouldn't it be better to go somewhere that people can actually hear you without all the interference? Well, that would be nice but the fact is you have to compete for the audience's attention along with everyone else. Everyone has to play, at least to an extent, in the same sphere as the others in their product category.

So what about direct sales (network marketing)? There is still competition. If your product line is shampoos and conditioners, then you're up against the likes of Procter & Gamble and Johnson & Johnson. You're wrestling with Suave, Paul Mitchell, Head and Shoulders, and a whole pantheon of other players.

If you want to sell cleaning products, you get to compete against Clorox, Windex, Mr. Clean, and another army. Selling cars? Look out for General Motors, Toyota, Ford, Nissan, Honda, BMW, and more.

Of course just because another business has already set up shop in your playground doesn't mean you can't beat them at their own game. The so-called home court advantage doesn't guarantee a victory. Then again, why play there if you don't have to? If you can sell a product that exists in its own space, why not go with the path of least resistance? In other words, you want your product to be unique. You want it to be different and new. You don't want to be selling the same thing as everyone else because then you have to convince all your customers that what you're selling isn't actually the same as everyone else. It's possible to convince customers that your product is revolutionary and better, but why saddle yourself with that tremendous burden? Why even go down that road?

The essential oil market is still fairly open. There are other players, to be sure, but they are few and far between and none of them is geared with the same culture as dōTERRA. Typically, dōTERRA's competitors' products are noticeably inferior in quality and they don't have sufficient distribution capacity or a system of training and education.

By selling a product that's unique in the marketplace you don't have to fight with other "musicians" to get audience attention. That means you get an express lane of customers coming straight to you. They aren't getting distracted by your competition. They can't buy it anywhere else…you are the source. Of course, being the sole source for a unique product also brings up another benefit of being unique: the concept of replacement or substitution.

When your product is truly unique it can't be replaced by something else. You can't, for instance, replace the tires on your car with something else. There are plenty of tire options out there but no options yet for 'tire alternatives.' Toilet paper is kind of the same way. There may be any number of brands, but there aren't many other options really.

Soda, on the other hand, has plenty of other options. You not only have all the different choices of soda, you also have juices, tea, coffee, smoothies, milk (in all its varieties), sports drinks, energy drinks, and, not the least, water. If you're planning on selling soda, be ready to struggle against all these different drink options plus the other soda manufacturers who sell the same flavors as you do.

In addition to being the only one (or at least one of the few) in your sphere, try to make sure that you don't overlap with another sphere. The point here is that there are plenty of potential customers out there, and you want to be able to capture as many of them as possible. The more unique and irreplaceable your product, the more people you'll be able to market to, and the less you'll have to fight to do it.

Desirable

Does anyone want to become the first network marketing professional to sell rapid-dissolving toilet paper? We're talking 'pull it off the roll and it's gone in 30 seconds' toilet paper. Can you imagine trying to sell that?

It's certainly unique, so it's got the first characteristic. It's also consumable (very consumable), however who wants to be the one *using* that product. No matter how much you educate people about the benefits to the septic system, they are going to be leery of something that might have so many other problems as side effects.

How about hair cream guaranteed to grow thick, black hair on any skin it touches? There's a market for that, but the number of bald people with thick, wavy black hair is narrow. You can't even sell to a customer with blond hair — or straight hair. Those customers won't want it.

Your product, therefore, should be desirable on its own merits. To decide whether your product qualifies, consider a thought experiment. Have you ever seen how people sometimes take items to the curb and leave them there with a sign saying "free"? How long does that stuff usually last? I suppose that depends on the street traffic, but most of the time those things don't last long unless they are really just garbage searching for a new dump. I've seen all kinds of things out on the curb including tables, chairs, TVs, bikes, sofas, cleaning products, etc. The nicer the condition of the item, the more quickly it tends to disappear.

Now the thought experiment: let's say you left a case of your product down on the curb. Would it disappear? How quickly would it disappear? Would one person take the whole thing, or would a series of people each take one?

At dōTERRA, our product is so good that it really would sell itself if we could just figure out a way to give it legs. Put a case of essential oils on the curb and I doubt you'd get more than a couple people driving by before the whole case was gone and probably all to the same person. The only reason that a person wouldn't want to buy essential oils is because that person doesn't yet understand the benefits. They don't cost enough to price people out of the market f—especially not in comparison to the value and benefits they bring. People just need to understand the value and benefits, which brings us to the importance of educating people about the value of your product. The easiest way to increase the desirability of your product is to educate your customer about it. You need to be the go-to source for information.

No one expects you to know everything about everything, but you need to be a gateway for your customer. If you don't know the answer, that's fine; you just need to be able to point the customer in the right direction and bring a correct answer on a future visit whenever possible.

I and my colleagues have been with dōTERRA long enough to know a lot of what there is to know about which oils to use for what ailments, at least for the common oils and common ailments. Of course there's much more to learn about the oils and we discover new uses and benefits all the time. But we didn't start with all that knowledge. Each time I shifted companies during my career, I basically had to start over. I went from whatever level of knowledge I had attained back to zero. That never deterred me, however, because I knew I could learn and I always made sure to get in touch with people who had the answers. If I couldn't answer a customer directly, I wanted to be able to put that customer in touch with a person who could. As you educate your customers they will come to trust you more. They will also come to understand the purpose and use for the product, making them more likely to buy it.

When I was starting out with the water filter company all those years ago, I made water my focus. I did so because it was easy to educate the customer about our water filtration product. It was easy to teach them how it worked and then show them the results. Once the customer went that far, they rarely backed out.

It's the same with any worthwhile product. With a little education, as long as there is real value in what you're sharing, most potential customers will buy it. Educating people about essential oils is easy. You just need to get the oils on them. Often, just smelling one of our oils will open up a person's mind and teach them the power of the oils in a way that no PowerPoint presentation could ever do. Having that experience will convert most people so it would be silly to try a different method.

At dōTERRA, we believe in experiential marketing, which means giving the customer the experience and then turning them loose. You'll see a return customer before long and the person will probably come back with others in tow. That's the power of a highly desirable and effective product.

Consumable

Let's do a little role-play. Imagine that you're finishing up with a customer and finally getting her order. Your product is a unique, highly desirable TV that actually blends into the wall when it's off. Turn it off and it basically becomes invisible. Pretty cool, huh? Because your company is fairly new, the TV also comes with a five-year warranty. That's a great selling point, isn't it?

You've been working this customer for about two months and she's finally decided that she is ready to place an order for a 60-inch TV for her living room. You're excited because that's a chunk of change in terms of your commission, and you've got bills to pay. You finalize all the paperwork, get her signed up, and get her check for the purchase price. You leave the house practically whistling with success and whistle all the way to the bank. Your hard work finally paid off. Good job.

Now, what's going to happen next month when you go back? Think she's going to want to buy again? What about next year? She's only got one living room. How long before you can realistically get her to buy again? Probably a decade, but it'll be at least five years. She's not going to need another TV until the one you just sold her breaks outside the warranty period.

There's a reason you don't usually see durable goods — appliances, TVs, cars, cameras, etc. — sold in a network marketing company. In the first place, items like those tend to be prohibitively expensive and have lots of competition. For another, there's no resale opportunity. Ideally, you want an affordable product. You'll notice that affordability isn't listed as one of the three traits because if people see the value, they'll buy anyway. The same can be true for your product, and it is for dōTERRA essential oils. There is value beyond the price tag.

That said, the higher the price tag, the harder it is to convince a customer of the value. What's more, you start to run into a situation where the customer is more likely to want to "think about it." Big purchases don't come easy to people. They have to mull it over for a while and weigh the pros and cons. Small purchases like that candy bar at the cash register are much easier to make as impulse purchases.

When was the last time you decided you needed a new refrigerator, car, computer, TV, or other big-ticket item and went right out and bought one? Did you really just walk into the first store, set your eyes on something, and buy it right then? I doubt it. You may have rushed the process but you likely still compared a couple of different options, weighed the price, and then made a decision. That's how big ticket purchases go and durable goods are more likely to be big ticket items. On the other hand, you probably didn't spend as much time agonizing over which box of cereal to buy, or which toilet paper. Consumables are more likely to fall under the "easy come, easy go" category and we're more likely to agree to buy them without spending long hours in contemplation beforehand.

When you're involved in network marketing, you want a product that people can decide about quickly. Products become prohibitively expensive when the customer has to stop and take some time to think about the decision. The specific price point is different from person to person, but the concept is the same across the board, and durable goods tend to be more expensive up front.

Additionally, if your product isn't consumable you won't be able to develop a customer relationship involving repeat buyers. Instead, you're going to have to widen your customer base and always be bringing in new customers. Car salesmen are always asking for referrals because they know you won't be back for years. Once they've sold to you, you're out of the market.

With consumables, the customer never leaves the pool of potential buyers for very long. If you stockpile something, you might be out of the pool for a while until you work through the stockpile, but you'll be back. That's why you want to sell products like juice, vegetables and toilet paper — things people use every day and use up in the process.

As awful as it sounds, you want your customers to run out of your product. Ideally, you'll keep them stocked enough that they don't ever actually run out, but you want them to have the chance. If you're selling exercise equipment, the customer can buy once and never buy again. If you're selling a nutritional supplement, the customer has to buy again.

A Caution

I want to point out that these three principles apply at all times, whether you like it or not. That's the nature of principles. Steven Covey tells us that a principle is timeless, universal, and in force whether you understand it and accept it or not.

Let me give you an example.

When my first networking company came crashing down, we shifted gears and went into selling templated Websites. Let's look at that product again to see which of these key traits it met. The Internet was in its infancy and there were hordes of companies trying to cash in on getting people onto the Web, both network marketing companies and more traditional ones. We were far from being unique. We were a dime-a-dozen provider of Web-hosting services and you could easily find a dozen other firms to provide what we offered.

There was nothing innately desirable about our product for a normal person like you and me. Sure, there was a market in the form of businesses and business owners, especially small business owners, but that market was much smaller than the market we were pursuing.

What use did a normal person have, back then, for a Website? Honestly, what use does a person have for a personal Website today? We have social media and blogs to fill that need for the average person like you and me. Websites are still the purview of businesses and organizations.

Finally, a Website isn't a consumable. It doesn't degrade every time a visitor comes to look at it. Websites might get old or stale over time in terms of styling and content, but they never really get used up. You can have a million visitors in a week or one visitor and the Website will still look the same at the end of the week.

Basically, our new product had none of the essential traits. We weren't unique, desirable, or consumable. There was no real reason that a person would want to buy in to our organization except for the fact that we had a really nice looking compensation structure. The only other reason to buy in was on the vague belief that the Internet would change everything and that you needed to get in on the ground floor or get left out forever. The Internet has changed everything, but it's just as easy to get on the Internet and break through today as it was back then with all the noise and chaos of its birth.

So, if our product had none of these three essential traits how were we successful with it? Well, it turns out that we were actually selling a different product. We weren't just selling Websites; they

● ● ●

were simply our cover story. What we were in fact selling was my team leader, let's call her Jennie, the woman I told you was so dynamic and great in front of an audience. I knew that if a customer came to Jennie's presentation, that customer was going to buy at the end. If Jennie told that customer to jump, the customer would do it. Jennie was just that good. She had a talent for influencing people. So I wasn't really selling templated Websites, and I wasn't teaching my team how to sell templated Websites either. We were selling Jennie, and she fit the three traits that every product needs to possess: She was definitely unique. There are plenty of great speakers in the world, but there is only one Jennie. You might be able to substitute another speaker in her place, but you can't recreate her exactly. She was highly desirable as a speaker. When she spoke, the room listened, and everyone felt something. She could fire up a crowd and get them going. Once people sat in front of her they were ready to do whatever she told them. Her skills meant that she was very inspiring, and everyone wants to be inspired. She was also consumable, in a sense. You could come to her seminar, learn, and be motivated, but you couldn't really take that home with you and put it on the mantle. If you wanted that same thing again, you had to come back to see her again the next month when she came back. Customers had to come back to her time and time again.

We were basically selling a motivational lecture series — courtesy of Jennie — and using the templated Websites as admission. If only I'd realized that at the time, I might have done things differently. Unfortunately, Jennie wasn't a product. You couldn't buy a can of distilled Jennie and the product that a customer was left with after listening to Jennie was basically worthless. It was not unique, desirable, or consumable. That fundamental issue is why the company failed.

The reason I bring this up is to point out the importance of selling the right product to the right person at the right price. If you're doing that, you are a salesperson with integrity. If you are selling the wrong product or selling to the wrong people or selling at the wrong price (or any combination of those things), you have violated your integrity.

Inadvertently, this is what we were doing when we were selling Jennie instead of a real product. The principles still worked, they just worked to the wrong ends. Since that time, I've always made sure to do my homework, to make sure I'm selling a product or service people actually need, not just selling a great sales pitch.

Exploding Your Business

If you're selling an actual product, and that product has all three of the essential qualities we have just discussed, as dōTERRA essential oils have, then you'll have a much easier time building your business. The product will basically take care of selling itself, which means you don't have to have persistent "salesmanship" as a natural talent. And, by selling a product instead of a person, including yourself, you can have success over the long-term.

Plenty of dōTERRA wellness advocates are normal people just like you and me. They don't have advanced degrees in marketing or anything else. They don't have 30 years of sales experience. They don't know the secrets to a quick close. Why? They don't need to. The product is unique and irreplaceable; it's highly desirable once a person has been educated a little about it; and it's consumable. The product sells itself over and over again. In fact, dōTERRA retains seven out of every 10 new customers. That's an extraordinary number. One of the industry giants in the health and beauty market retains about one out of every 10 customers. That tells me that they need to work seven times more to achieve the same results. It also tells me that we've got a great product. The national average for customer retention for direct sales companies is only two out of 10. That means the average network marketing professional needs to work three and a half times as much as the average dōTERRA wellness associate.

I attribute this success to the product, hands down. I don't know how many times I've been in an event and asked who has ever tried network marketing before. Usually, about half the hands go up. Then I follow up by asking who swore they'd never try it again. Most of the same hands go up. Then I ask them "Then why are you here?" The answer is the product. Our essential oils are life changing and it doesn't take much experience for people to learn that. Once they do, that conversion runs deep.

Other network marketing companies have decent products but many of them aren't actually in business to sell product. For some of them their real product is actually their business and compensation plan, not what they're selling. That's why network marketing can get a bad name at times. Too many companies out there would sell chalk in a plastic bag if they could get away with it.

At dōTERRA, we believe in a high quality product with real, tangible benefits. We believe in changing lives, and our numbers show it. Having such a great product means we don't need to be sneaky to trick people into buying. We can just be honest with them. Our wellness advocates don't need to know the ins and outs of the quick close. They can just talk to people like a regular person. In other words, having the right product means you can focus on all the other aspects of the business because you don't have to worry about the sales aspect. You still need to find new clients, but you can turn them into repeat customers with less effort, leaving you more time to find more new customers and focus on self-improvement.

Again, it's possible to make a living off products that don't have all three of these characteristics but it means more work for you. You'll have to fight more competition, use more salesmanship, or find more customers to make the same success. You can still do it, but it means you're planning on more of a struggle.

Given the choice, I'd pick the product that sells itself so I can focus on everything else in the business. That's the simplest path to success.

3. Vital Behaviors

"Never tell people how to do things. Tell them what to do and they will surprise you with their ingenuity." —General George Patton

Once people know they have an appropriate product to sell, the next question they always ask me is, "How do I build this business?" The answer is that "how" doesn't matter. The real question to answer is "Why?" As in "Why do I want to build this business?" If you can answer that question, you'll be well on your way to having outstanding success, according to your own definition of success. I could teach you how to be successful at network marketing in half an hour or so. That's all it would take to give you a chance to learn all the necessary skills. In fact, that's what this chapter is about. I'm going to teach you the behaviors necessary to have success in the network marketing profession. But before we get there, I need to make sure you understand your "why" – otherwise the "how" won't matter.

Hopefully, no one is still reading this who is hoping for easy money. Network marketing — legitimate, product-based network marketing — isn't about "getting rich quick." In many cases it isn't even about "getting rich slow," because it isn't about "getting rich" at all. For many people, network marketing is about success outside the financial realm. It's a means to an end.

Many people are tired of their commute, or boss, or coworkers or vacation schedule. They want the flexibility of making ends meet on their own terms or the chance to spend more time with family. For someone like that, the presidential diamond club isn't the goal. The goal is income replacement so that they can free up their time and be more flexible in how they allocate that time. Why you want to get into network marketing is more important than how you are going to do it. If you're only in it for the cars, trips, and fame, you are far less likely to stick with it when the going gets tough. And trust me, the going will get tough from time to time — it's the nature

● ● ●

of business…any business.

That's why I always encourage people to be sure of their "why" before they start. Have your reasons, and remind yourself of those reasons often. Otherwise, a time will come when it will be too easy to skip the "how to" in favor of something else and that's usually something that seems to provide a more direct route to your "why." Your reasons, your "why," will give you the motivation to stick with the program when the simple things turn out to be less easy than you originally anticipated. They'll give you the motivation to do the "hows" of network marketing.

The how-to of networking marketing are actually quite simple. There are just a few vital behaviors you need to develop:
Use the product yourself.
Share the product with others.
Promote the product through promotional events.

If you'll do just these few things, and do them consistently, you'll have success. It's that simple, although as we have already discussed that doesn't mean it's easy.

Use and Share the Product

If you want success you first have to use the product. When you use the products, you'll build a set of experiences to share with others, adding to your credibility and effectiveness.

The second vital behavior is almost an extension of the first one: share the product with other people. After you are sharing with yourself, you're ready to share with others. In fact, you have to share with others. You can be the best wellness advocate in the entire universe and never make a penny if you won't open your mouth and talk to people. Conversely, you can be the worst in the universe and still have plenty of success if you'll just talk to everyone. Your rate of success is really determined by your skill as a sharer, whether your product has the three essential traits or not, and how many people you talk to. Having great strength in one of those areas can help to make up for weakness in one of the others. Being strong in all three will accelerate your progress.

If you have a stellar product, it'll sell itself, as we've discussed. However, it's still up to you to open your mouth and share it with someone else. If you won't talk to people, you won't be able to share the benefits of your product with them. So, if you have a good product and you're willing to talk to a lot of people, you don't necessarily need "salesmanship" to have success. The product will sell itself, and you'll give it lots of opportunities to do so by merely sharing it with others. That's why salesmanship is not one of the vital behaviors. If you've picked a good product, you don't need salesmanship. You just need to give the product plenty of opportunities to shine.

Of course, that doesn't mean it's easy. Talking to friends and family, trying to get them to buy a product from you is never easy. Doing the same with strangers may be easier or harder for you, but it's still a challenge. You have to be ready for those who'll tell you "No thanks." In the case of dōTERRA, sharing is as easy as having the potential customer put oil on. Put a couple drops in their hand and let them have that experience. Mission accomplished. For other products, and especially services, it may not be as easy. Still, recognize your place as being something other than a salesperson. You aren't there to push product on people. That ends up pushing people away no matter how good your product is. You're sharing something of value with people you like, and if they decide it has value for them, they know where they can get some.

I had an experience on a nice vacation in Hawaii with my wife that demonstrates this point perfectly. We were staying in a nice hotel — one of an international chain of hotels —and ended up in a "conversation" with a gentleman about the opportunity to secure future stays at a discount at the whole range of different resorts around the world. Because of my background in sales and networking I saw the conversation for what it was almost right away, but I didn't say anything because I've always loved watching people's approaches to sales. Keri didn't catch it quite as quickly, however. She continued to listen and you could see that she was giving thought to what the man was saying. Then the man tipped his hand and her walls went up. I watched the light of realization come on in her eyes as she shut down. After that, there was nothing that man could say or do to renew her interest, but it was entertaining to watch him try.

Most people are like Keri. They may not know it at a conscious level, but they are ready to shut down the moment they catch on to a sale's pitch. That's doubly true in the case of network marketing and direct sales.

When you go to the appliance store or the car dealership, you expect someone to try to sell you, and you're a little more forgiving and open when it happens. When you're talking to someone in the line at the grocery store, you aren't so accepting. You'll shut down more quickly and decisively at the first glimmer of a sale's approach. So you can't promote the product by selling the product. If you try that method, you'll lose more fish than you ever hook. However, if you can let your product do the talking and then follow up with an opportunity to learn more about the business, the customer has already had the product experience, so they remain open because you're promoting what they have already enjoyed using.

My recommendation is to make two new contacts and two follow-up contacts each day, Monday through Friday. You don't need to recruit hundreds of people each week, just share your product with 10 new people each week and follow up with 10 people who have already sampled the product. Do this consistently and you will develop a massive sales team to work with you.

"Meeting" is a Four-Letter Word

The third vital behavior is to educate people about the product through promotional events. Some people are absolutely great at promoting events; others have no idea what this even means. The idea is that sharing the product with someone, when done properly, is like providing a baited hook. Once a potential customer has experienced it, they are ready for the next level.

Next they need to gain an education about the product or service, and that requires an opportunity to attend classes and receive instruction. That happens at events and your job is to become good at explaining to people the value of events and helping them to get there.

The first step in becoming an expert promoter of meetings is to avoid using the word "meeting." That's right. No more setting up "meetings" with people. Nobody responds well to the word "meeting." The reasoning behind this is interesting and goes back to the various times in our lives when we've experienced meetings. For those of us who have ever had a full-time job, we likely experienced meetings in the workplace. In most cases, those meetings were opportunities to bring lots of people together to sit around and accomplish little to nothing. Often, meetings become forums for argument, frustration, and offense. Traditionally, only half an agenda gets covered in a meeting, while dozens of unrelated, spurious topics come up and consume all the time. Everyone leaves the meeting feeling confused and ignored. Very few people feel like their important points were heard and even fewer feel like anything worthwhile happened. In fact, companies all over the world are instituting different techniques like standing meetings or 15-minute "power" meetings to improve the effectiveness of their meetings and improve productivity. Unless you want to absorb all the negative baggage associated with people's experiences with work meetings, I'd recommend you use a different term. In addition, when you ask someone to come to a meeting and they know you're in network marketing, they automatically think they don't want to get involved until they realize they actually do. People have often had experiences with other network-marketing-opportunity introductory meetings. These experiences were not usually positive.

Very few of the top producers I know have had any real prior experience with being successful at another network marketing company. At these other companies people typically experience being bullied into buying product they don't need and aren't sure how to sell. They are frontloaded (which we'll talk about more in the next chapter), and then abandoned.

As you can imagine (if you haven't already experienced this yourself) being sold a starter pack and then left alone to figure out how to move the product is frustrating. When people have that experience they associate it back to the persuasive speaker and all the wonderful things they were told at that meeting. From that point on the person doesn't like the idea of going to another meeting for a network marketing opportunity.

Timeshares are another version of these meetings. Nearly everyone has been roped into a meeting like this at one time or another. You sit and listen to people drone on and on about a great deal on something you don't really want or can't actually afford. It's a total waste of your time. The main reason you went was because of the "sea vessel" they were giving you for your time, which turned out to be a plastic inner tube with a couple of rope loops on the sides.

So, you can see that the word "meeting" has a lot of usages, and most of them aren't positive. Unless you want to saddle your event with all the baggage associated with the word "meeting," you should probably find a different word to use. You can use words like event, class, or even party, but be careful which word you choose.

"Event" is sufficiently vague that you can get away with calling almost anything an event. At the same time, however, there is a sense of mystique, intrigue, and urgency associated with the word. Because of its broad range of uses, the word event is a great choice when you're planning.

Another option is to call your meeting a class. This is equally appropriate to calling it an event so long as some form of instruction will take place. Now, can I tell you a secret? Some form of instruction should be taking place regardless of what you call the gathering. No matter what you call your event, when people come together and give you their time, they'd better get something in return or they won't be willing to give you their time again in the future. If you host a class and teach them something they didn't know before, you've given them something in return for their time. No matter what you call the gathering, you need to make sure that your attendees come away enriched somehow.

A third option is to call your event a party. There's some draw to doing this because the word party is associated with fun and food and mingling and other social wonderfulness. You might be able to increase your attendance by calling your gathering a party, however, be very careful that you actually hold a party if you choose to tell people you're holding a party. Can you imagine hearing about a party and getting all ready to go? You're excited and ready to mingle. You're ready to have some fun. Then you show up to find a room full of folding chairs and a projector at the head of the room. For the next hour you are taught about a product or business opportunity, and then everyone packs up and goes home. How are you feeling about that party? How do those feelings rub off onto whatever product or service you just learned about? Would you even stay until the end? Maybe you'd stay in hopes that the party is after the class, right? So be careful when calling your gathering a party. If you're going to call it that, you need to actually have a party. You need to have time for people to mix and mingle. You need to make provision for music and food. You might consider some games or other activities.

I've found that the easiest thing to do is to just call a spade a spade and refer to your gathering as an event or class. You're definitely holding an event, and the event usually takes the form of an interactive class, so those two names seem to work best. Still, it's up to you to make your events what you will, and then name them accordingly.

Whatever you call your event, don't forget: the magic happens after the class when people have the opportunity to experience the product and ask questions one on one. So if the magic is after the meeting, get to the "after meeting" quicker. And remember to keep it simple, and keep it short. Introduction classes should be 45 minutes or less, and the after meeting can be as long as people are interested in hanging around.

Promoting Events

Once you know what to call the event, you need to promote it to others if you want to have a successful gathering. You best way to promote your event is to ask people directly. A face-to-face contact has always been the best way to secure a commitment, but it's not the only way.

In addition to face-to-face contacts, you can reach out via social media and publicize the event. You can also create fliers or handouts and spread them around. Email is another tool for inviting people, but email isn't a very effective way to drum up interest — especially for new customers.

The problem with email is that we all get so much of it that most of it gets filtered out and never looked at. Even the emails that make it through spam filters are deleted before they're opened as often as not. If the email does get opened, most people will skim it briefly, look at any pictures, and then delete it. If you don't grab their attention in those three seconds, they won't really be paying attention to the fact that you're hosting a class. Email tends to be more effective with established customers. When you have an existing relationship, email is a great way to communicate. It's simple and nonintrusive. However, for a new customer it's not enough of a connection to garner much attention. For new customers, you need a more personal approach, like a face-to-face invitation.

Another advantage of the face-to-face invitation is that it gives you a chance to share a product sample and stir interest with that customer. It also gives the customer a chance to see your commitment and enthusiasm.

Phone calls work but cold calling doesn't work as well. You're more likely to come off as a telemarketer in a cold call. When you're calling an existing connection, you're more likely to seem genuine because you already have that relationship.

I wouldn't recommend putting an ad in the paper. That worked 20 years ago when I was getting started, but very few people get the paper anymore and many who do don't really read it.

However you choose to contact and invite people, there are a couple additional techniques to increasing attendance. The first is to send out text message or email reminders the day before. If your customers are more relaxed, you might even send out a reminder a few days before and then again on the day before. Sending a reminder reinforces your commitment and helps build a sense of importance and urgency, which we'll talk about in a moment. Some people will honestly just forget that they were going to go. Getting that reminder will reduce your number of accidental no-shows.

Finally, the old adage "pick them up, and they'll show up" holds true here. If you really want someone to attend an event, pick them up for it. It's easy for people to skip a class when they are responsible for getting there on their own. Any number of things can come up to dampen their enthusiasm at that last, critical moment. If you arrange to pick them up, however, they're much less likely to give you an excuse for why they can't attend when you're standing on their doorstep. And, if they do give you an excuse, it's more likely to be a good one, and they're more likely to call ahead and tell you rather than just being a no show.

Earning Interest

As you promote your event and share it with everyone, you need to also work to generate interest in the event. This is what will transition people from simply being aware of the event to building a desire to attend. One of the ways to do this is to help potential customers see how attendance can be rewarding; another is to create a sense of urgency.

You should be up front with your potential customers about any door prizes or other incentives that will be available at the event. People are motivated by incentives, so providing some kind of tangible reward for their attendance will make your event look like a more appealing alternative to another night in front of the TV. When you show how your guests will be compensated for their time, you help to offset the pull of other, less-profitable activities.

If you think that giving away door prizes sounds too expensive, keep in mind that things you give away to promote your business (incentives, samples, informational materials) count as business expenses and lower your tax burden. So talk about that with your accountant and see what kind of advantages you can gain by giving out door prizes.

Another way to build interest is through creating a sense of urgency for your customers. The last time you had an urgent need to go to the grocery store was probably because you were out of something you needed in order to make dinner that night. Otherwise, grocery stores run sales for a week or more at a time, and they run sales all the time. There's no urgency to rush over when a new sale is announced. Contrast that with Black Friday after Thanksgiving. Everyone mobs the retail outlets to take advantage of the one-day only sales, door busters, and other incentives. Ironically, research shows that Black Friday deals aren't the best deals of the holiday shopping season. They may be good deals, but they aren't the best ones. Still, that "sense" of urgency created by the stores drives people to go out and shop. So, if you have someone come and present every Thursday you don't need to say it that way to your prospective customer. Don't lie, obviously, but you don't need to emphasize the lack of urgency either. For example, don't say, "I've got a gentleman who comes and gives a presentation on the basics of the product every week. He's doing it Thursday this week. Do you want to come?" Instead, you can say something more along the lines of, "There's an amazing educator coming into town to give a class on natural wellness; you've got to be there."

No matter how often your speaker comes and gives the identical presentation, make it seem like it's unique so that customers feel a sense of urgency about it. Otherwise, they'll tell themselves that they can wait for the next meeting...or the next...or the next.

In other words, they'll never show up because they'll always be putting it off for a more convenient time.

Building Commitment

Ultimately, you want as many people at your events as you can get. The larger your audience is, the better your chances of finding new customers and even enrolling someone on your team. In any group, you'll find a certain percentage of early adopters, a percentage of wait-and-see-ers and a percentage of naysayers. The early adopters will enroll right away. The other two groups won't. The wait-and-see-ers will need more time and proof before they're willing to commit, and you shouldn't waste your time on the naysayers. If they come around it won't be through your efforts; it will be because they had a life-changing event that opened them up to new possibilities.

Depending on the strength of your product and the composition of your audience, you may not need a very large class. If your product has the three essential traits, and you bring enough samples to go around, you should be able to secure quite a few enrollments. Still, the best course of action is to just invite everyone and make sure the venue is big enough to accommodate them.

The best way to invite people is by giving them an experience with your product. We've found that the likelihood of someone attending an event goes up dramatically if they've had a positive product experience beforehand. Once they've had that experience, they'll go to the event because they want to learn more about something that already helps them. People aren't as likely to show up to your event if they haven't had that experience first. It just won't be as important to them. They'll ignore the event because they see it as an opportunity to learn more about something that doesn't matter anyway; *i.e.*, they'll see your event as a waste of their time. It would be like reeling in your line before the fish has taken the bait. We call this concept of sampling the product first experiential marketing (though it sometimes feels like experimental marketing), and we've had a lot of success with it. When people get a chance to sample the product they build an internal reason to believe in the product. That internal reason is built totally independent of you and your biases and opinions so the reason will carry more weight.

One of the surest ways to get people to commit is to help them find their own reason. No persuasion you can supply will ever be as strong as a reason they come to on their own. That's just human nature. Anything anyone else tells us is always suspect. Anything we tell ourselves is the foundation of reality.

That may sound a little harsh or even sarcastic, but that's how the world works. We make our own reality in the same way we make our own success, and your customers and distributors will be more focused and devoted if they are crafting their own realities to include your product. If you attempt to do all the persuading on your own, their faith will be shaken the moment you either don't know an answer or give a wrong answer. Don't make people build on you as a foundation. Give them the product and let them build their own foundation. If you really want them to attend an event, you will need to help them build that initial foundation as soon as possible. That means giving them a chance to build their own experiences with the product. Everything else will be based on that.

No Fire-hosing

Once you get people at your event you want to make sure they have a good time. We'll talk about this more in the section on Presentation Skills, but the idea is that you want to give them useful information without overloading them.

You will have more knowledge about your product or service than your customer will want or need. You will know more about your business than your customer will. You have so much to share with those customers, so, what should you share? The complication you will face is that all of the information you have is important. So how do you determine what's most important for a diverse audience? The key is to stick with the basics in group settings and focus on specific needs in individual settings.

We all know the expression "trying to drink from a fire hose." Typically, the expression is used to describe a situation in which you're trying to absorb far more information than you ever possibly could. Depending on the scenario, the fire hose approach is usually an uncomfortable, frustrating one. We don't like being overwhelmed by new things.

First of all, we don't like to be bombarded with so much information all at once because it makes us feel stupid. We secretly wonder how there could be a subject out there that we know so little about and that makes us uncomfortable. You never want to say or do something that will make a customer like himself less.

Secondly, when we're inundated with so much information all at once, we can be overwhelmed by how far behind we feel. Rather than seeing the steps to get from where we are to where we want to go, all we see is this vast wall of knowledge, and we get intimidated. You never want to intimidate your customers.

Now, none of us goes out and intentionally fire-hoses another person. We don't mean to blast people away with the pressure of so much new information. We do it because we're so excited, and that excitement is a good thing. You want that enthusiasm, and you want others to see it, but you have to display it at the right time and in the right way.

When I was just getting started in networking I made the mistake of fire-hosing my brother. I was so excited about what we were doing and the opportunity and potential that I came on too strong. I ended up blasting him back more than a year (it was a year before I could really talk to him about the opportunity again). Learn from my mistake and keep the classes simple; stick to the basics. We can all use reinforcement on the basics, no matter our current experience, and you won't scare away as many new customers and distributors that way.

You also want to avoid intimidation because any kind of coercion or fear is a very quick way to end a new relationship. Family and friends will resent you if you try to push them around, and new customers will just leave. So keep it simple and understandable and let people come to you with their deeper questions. They'll be more satisfied when they can get the information they want at their own pace, rather than having it force fed to them.

Sealing the Deal

One of the keys to success is to put away the tactics of coercion and trickery and just focus on the customer's needs instead. Even if you stick to the basics and keep things simple, not everyone will want to get started. In part, this is because about half of the population just isn't wired for entrepreneurship. These people can still be candidates to use your product, but they'll require special attention to help them be successful as part of your organization.

Regardless of whether a person is wired for the self-motivated entrepreneurship route or the employee route, there are some phrases you can use to increase your odds of success. Just like with the word "meeting," certain words and phrases should be avoided while others should be used.

First of all, don't ever use the phrases "join" or "sign up." We're programmed to put up an all out salesman-defense wall when we hear those words. I don't care how amazing your product or business structure is; if you ask someone to sign up they will be far less likely to follow through. That's just human behavior.

We've all seen far too many scams asking us to sign up for something in order to get something else. We've all seen different clubs you can join to get music or movies or something else and the horror stories that usually follow. However, thanks to institutions like Sam's Club and Costco, nearly everyone in America knows the value of having a membership with a place where goods can be purchased at wholesale prices. So, rather than signing someone up to be a distributor, consider rephrasing your invitation: **"Would it be okay if I showed you how to set up your wholesale membership?"**

There are several important components to this question.

First, there is verifiable power in the phrase "Would it be okay if….?" The nature of the human mind is that by the time you finish those words the other party will already be agreeing in his or her mind without even knowing what you're asking for yet. As long as your request doesn't end up being something unreasonable people will agree to what you're saying. Why? Because you are giving them the power but also putting them in a position where they will have to be rude in the use of that power to say "no." If someone is legitimately not interested, that person will decline no matter how you phrase things and you can move on.

Of course, this only works if you maintain that power structure throughout the rest of the exchange, so it isn't something you can fake. You have to be genuine about wanting what's best for the customer. The way this most frequently comes up is in terms of the enrollment package. You have to maintain your nonthreatening, no coercive approach, or you'll burn up all the good will you just earned. So, rather than pushing them to sign up for a large, expensive package to start out with, allow the customer to choose the best fit. At dōTERRA, for instance, we have a starter kit for under $30, and then on up to the diamond package at over $2,000, and we have a number of different packages in between. But you don't even have to push the product packages. If a customer wants to enroll with a single bottle of lemon oil for $10, I'd let her.

Don't focus on your commission from what they order. Just focus on the customer's needs and readiness. If you give a positive experience to your new customers, they'll come back and order more. Soon.

When I enroll someone I emphasize that there are a number of different methods for enrolling. I also point out that I don't so much care if they enroll right away. In fact, I don't care how, when, or where they enroll, so long as they do enroll. I explain that to my new customers to take the pressure out of the situation. As humans, we have a natural desire to be in control of ourselves. If I push you to do something, you're going to instinctively want to resist me, even if I'm pushing you to do something you want to do anyway.

If you've given a good presentation and made yourself available to answer questions, the customer's interest will be there. It's up to you at that point to maintain that interest and not diminish it. You have to give that power and control back to the customer and the customer will act on that interest in turn.

Choose Your Words Carefully

Another way to give this control back to the customer is to empower the customer in the way you say things. One of the key phrases for empowering customers is "You know how…." The concept behind this phrase is that it puts an idea in the person's head as though that idea always belonged to the person. This happens either through triggering memory recall (she really did know the information already) or because none of us want to admit that we didn't know something, so we convince ourselves that we already did (she'll fool herself into believing she already knew the information).

Either way, this technique allows you to supply information in a nonthreatening way so that your audience can all be on the same page with you. For instance, "You know how side effects from pharmaceutical drugs kill more people than car accidents every year." This introductory statement is a bit shocking for people who don't know it already, but the nature of the words will help them accept it and follow along. For the people who *do* already know, the statement serves to put them in the right frame of mind for what you're going to talk about next.

Another example relates to helping people see the value of automatic ordering. Every network marketing company I've encountered has a way to ship product every month without the customer needing to repeatedly place the order. Frequently, the automatic nature of the order will earn the customer a small discount but the practice of an automatic ordering program is pretty standard. Enrolling your customers (and distributors) in your auto-ship program is a great way to ensure that you will make a little income each month. It's also a great way for your customers to make sure that they don't run out of the products they use.

At dōTERRA the program is called Loyalty Rewards and I try to get everyone set up for it whenever possible. To do so I explain: "Loyalty Rewards is the most intelligent method of ordering product from the company."

That may sound a little forced, but it's a true statement. If a company offers a discount on its products, the most intelligent way to order is to order with that discount. If you're going to order the product anyway, why not buy it at the lowest possible price? What's more, explaining the program this way does something in the customer's head: instead of just asking the customer to sign up for Loyalty Rewards, you've edified the customer. You've given the customer a chance to be intelligent. When you phrase your invitation this way, the little man inside that customer's head is going to go upstairs and turn on the lights. After all, who doesn't want to consider himself to be intelligent? If you are proposing the most intelligent way to do things, then your customers will want to do things in that way to reinforce their own intelligence.

Thankfully, this isn't a manipulative gimmick because it's actually true. Loyalty Rewards really *is* the most intelligent method for ordering from dōTERRA, and telling people about a way to save money is an attempt on your part to do something nice—even if it's also true that it's something nice for you.

The Art of Not Quitting

In the end, these vital behaviors are simple enough, but sadly, many people will quit before they see success. Why? Because it's just as easy — if not easier — to *not* do the vital behaviors as it is to do them. It's easy to *not* share the product. It's easy to *not* invite people to an upcoming class and to *not* promote the event.

Add to that the fact that quitting is something of a Great American Pastime. America was once the golden land of opportunity where doers could come and make something of themselves, come hell or high water. The nation was carved out of wilderness, mostly without the advantages of the cars, airplanes, and heavy machinery we enjoy today. Today's luxury, however, has come at a price. Life used to be hard work, day in and day out, or you died. Today, with a little government assistance, you can get by without lifting a finger. When life can be so easy why would anyone want to go the hard route?

So we quit school, we quit jobs, we quit exercise routines, we quit marriages, and we quit life. One of the few things that we universally *don't* quit is complaining. I once heard it said that half the population is already dead; they're just waiting for the coroner's report to confirm it. That was obviously a joke, but there's a frightening ring of truth to it.

Of course, as often as not, we don't realize we are quitting because we rarely quit anything cold turkey. That's too hard to justify — especially when it's something we know we should be doing (like school, work, exercise, or relationships). Instead, we quit with one compromise at a time. We disengage slowly until we can erase all the reasons why we started something in the first place.

This happens with school and work when we start to complain about our professors or bosses. We build those walls, disengage with what's going on, and slowly exit. The same holds true with marriage. We stop looking at our spouse's virtues and begin focusing on the vices. We engage in open dialogue less and less often until there's nothing left to talk about. Then, in very little time, the relationship is dead and it's easy to walk away.

The same process holds true in the networking profession. Thankfully, because people tend to follow the same path to the exit, you can diagnose them and head them off. You can also diagnose yourself and get yourself re-engaged.

The first indication that a person is quitting network marketing is that they stop sharing the product, either because they get too busy or too tired. They stop sharing the product with others. This leads to an empty calendar, which is much easier to walk away from than a list of appointments.

As people stop sharing, they also stop coming to events. Here, again, the concept of progressive withdrawal holds true. People generally don't come to events faithfully and then stop all at once. That happens, but it's usually for some glaring ideological break or other momentous life change. For most quitters, the process is less dramatic, though no less drastic.

Rather than stopping cold turkey, people will miss a meeting then attend the next. They'll be on and off again for a while but with an ever-decreasing rate of attendance. Then, eventually, they'll drop out entirely. At some point during or after this process, they'll cancel their personal order. While they may retain a faith in the products or services, having that personal order will be a constant reminder of their failure, and none of us wants that kind of reminder.

This slow fade might be tough to notice in its early stages, but you need to address it the moment you recognize it. The earlier you take corrective steps — especially for yourself — the less ground you'll lose. It will also be that much easier to get yourself back on track and moving forward. So, to an extent, you have to be constantly on your guard and constantly pushing back against that motivation to disconnect. Everyone feels the drive to quit on a regular basis, but you can choose whether to act on the impulse or to stick it out through the hard times.

Let me emphasize here that when I'm talking about the problem of quitting, I'm talking about the *act* of quitting, not the *desire* to quit. We all feel a drive to quit when we run into something difficult. That's a natural response because it means we're going to have to put forth extra effort; however, our instinct is to conserve energy for when that saber-tooth cat jumps out and starts running at us. So don't feel bad if you are constantly plagued with the desire to quit things. That's normal. In fact, if you don't want to quit one thing or another at least twice a week you're probably not doing very much. If you never feel the drive to quit, you probably aren't doing anything difficult, which means you aren't pushing yourself to stretch and grow.

You'll be tempted to quit quite frequently in network marketing because this is a get-rich-slow profession. You're going to have to stick it out through the hard days over the long-term before you find deep, lasting success. For that reason, I'll make you a deal: you can quit anytime you want so long as you quit on a good day. If it's been a good day for you and your business, you can quit, if you want. If it's been a bad day for you or the business you need to postpone your decision to quit (or not) until you have a good day again.

Start starting and quit quitting.

Imagine, for a moment, the impact this one, simple rule would have on society. Think of the marriages that could be saved, the jobs that could be retained, and the education that could be earned. All it would take is an agreement to not quit in the thick of thin things. Instead, if we focus on our "whys" we'll be able to remember why we got involved in something so difficult in the first place. We'll be able to motivate ourselves to keep moving even when it's hard. This is when it becomes a big advantage to have a vision board or some other list of goals and aspirations. A list in your head doesn't really count.

The Doubling Penny

You need that strong "why" because it's so easy to give up otherwise. It's so easy to *not* make your contacts, order your product, and promote events. It's much easier to give up than go out on a limb and share with new people, especially when you consider that network marketing, when done correctly, is the opposite of "get rich quick."

Network marketing is the great equalizer in the sense that anyone and everyone can get rich at it. In fact, Donald Trump was once asked what he would do tomorrow if he lost his fortunes today. He said that he would go into MLM (multi-level marketing; *i.e.,* network marketing) because anyone could make millions that way.

• • •

That's a big endorsement for all the networking professionals in the world, but there's more to it than that. He never said anyone could make millions *quickly* because, the truth is, it's not a quick process. Also, he said "anyone *could*" make millions, not that "everyone *does*." The fact of the matter is that most people *don't* get rich in network marketing because they don't ever push themselves to that level — they quit before they get there. In fact, if everyone *did* get rich in the networking profession, there would be very few other professions left. The difficulty is that networking can be a slow business. You have to build relationships before you can have success and that takes time and effort.

Allow me to give you an illustration of the cumulative effect of building something slowly — especially at first. If I offered you your choice between $1 million or a penny that doubled every day for 30 days, which would you choose? Of course, between the section heading and being offered the choice, you're trying to second guess me about which is the better option. Well, given the actual choice in real life most people would choose the million. Why? Because it's easy and immediate. You don't have to think about it. You know what a million dollars is worth, so it's an easy decision to make. However, it's the wrong decision.

With the doubling penny, you get far more money. Five times as much money, in fact; but it's hard to see that at the beginning of the process. So let me put up some values here, and you can follow along to see the difference. I'm not going to list all 30 days, but I'll share the beginning, middle and end so you can get a feel for what's happening.

Day	Million Dollars	Doubling Penny
1	$1,000,000.00	$0.01
2	$1,000,000.00	$0.02
3	$1,000,000.00	$0.04
4	$1,000,000.00	$0.08
...		

14	$1,000,000.00	$81.92
15	$1,000,000.00	$163.84
16	$1,000,000.00	$327.68
17	$1,000,000.00	$655.36
...		
27	$1,000,000.00	$671,088.64
28	$1,000,000.00	$1,342,177.28
29	$1,000,000.00	$2,684,354.56
30	$1,000,000.00	$5,368,709.12

Amazing, isn't it? This illustration is designed to show the power of compounding interest, but I have never found a better example to illustrate the realities of the network marketing business. Notice that the doubling penny doesn't become the better choice until day 28, almost the very end. For 93 percent of the month the million is the better choice. With the doubling penny, you don't even clear $10,000 until day 21, two-thirds of the way through the month. How disheartening is that?

When you look around and see people with their "normal" jobs and "normal" success —their million dollars — it can be very tempting to want to give up on the doubling penny process — on the networking profession — and follow after them. Look again, however, at where you end up. The 30 days in the illustration obviously don't equate to 30 days in the real world in terms of work (how many jobs pay you $1 million up front for your work?) and that just adds to the frustration. Your 30 days could be months or even years. Depending on how diligent you are to the vital behaviors we discussed, you might never reach the end of your 30 days. That's why I share this example. I've seen too many people quit right at the tipping point.

In my experience, people tend to quit in the 14-18 day range. They've worked hard, they've seen some success, but they feel like the success isn't coming quickly enough. They feel like they're being outpaced by the people around them — especially the people who got theirs right up front.

At that point, they falter in their resolve and their vital behaviors start to slip. They stop sharing the product as often. They stop promoting events. They start cleaning up their resumes and looking for "real" jobs. As they lose focus, their progress slips and their 30 days stretches even further into the future. Eventually they give up — right on the cusp of the real growth and success.

I've seen it happen far too many times and it breaks my heart. If they would just stick it out a bit longer they'd see the larger gains from the later days. Just think about it. It takes 20 days to hit that first $10,000. In the next 10 days, however, you go from $10,000 to $5.3 million. The reason networking works this way is because it takes a lot of time and faithful effort to lay the foundation for your business. You have to build out the network that will sustain you. You have to constantly nourish and grow your customer and distributor base, re-investing every spare penny back into the business (which we'll talk about later). Then, finally, after all that work, the foundation will be laid and the base will be strong enough to start rewarding you for all your work. That's when you finally hit those last few days and realize the success you've been working toward all along. So don't quit when the success starts off slowly. Stick with it. The vital behaviors are simple enough to do, just keep on doing them and over time you'll start to see your success accelerate, then rocket upward. The key is to just keep with the vital behaviors. There's nothing fancy or complex about them. Just stick with the simple formula of these behaviors and you'll reach your day 30!

4. Duplication

"That which we persist in doing becomes easier for us to do; not that the nature of the thing itself has changed, but that our power to do is increased." — *Ralph Waldo Emerson*

We've established that the things you need to do as a networking professional are simple. We've also established that they may not be easy to do but that their ease (or difficulty) has no bearing on the simplicity of the individual tasks and that the difficulty usually stems from the fact that it's just as easy to *not* do the simple things as it is *to* do them.

We then talked about the three traits your product needs to have and the three behaviors you need to follow for success. Now I want to reinforce all of that by telling you the secret —right here in the fourth chapter — of finding success in the network marketing profession. The secret is "duplication." Much like the instructions on the shampoo bottle of, "Lather, rinse, repeat," that's what you need to be doing in network marketing to be successful. Duplication is the mother of everything in the networking profession. The concept is exceptionally simple: find what works and keep doing it over and over. This is the concept that "if it ain't broke, don't fix it." You don't need to spend time and effort to come up with new approaches and new techniques if you're already doing what works. Once you know what works, just do it again and again until the environment changes to a point that the technique doesn't work anymore.

If you're creating an effective, principle-based technique it should be something that can be duplicated by the other members of your team as well, and it shouldn't ever really wear out. It should continue to work for as long as you want it to.

In terms of what you should be duplicating, let me break down network marketing into its absolute, simplest form. For a moment, I'm going to set aside all the training programs, sales techniques, product benefits, paradigm and philosophy material, and everything else. Put away everything you've ever learned for just a moment and let me give you the key to success in just three simple steps:

1. Use the product.
2. Teach others to use the product.
3. Repeat steps 1 and 2 (in other words, duplicate).

Use, teach, duplicate. It's really that simple. You can see how the three essential traits plug into this simple process too. The product or service needs to have the three traits if you're going to want to use it for yourself, and then you need to share the product and promote events to teach others how to use the product, too. After that, it's just a matter of starting over and doing it again and again until you've achieved the level of success that you desire.

Does this sound too good to be true? That's because it's simple. In fact, it's so simple that your mental estimation of the time and effort required is probably at odds with the simplicity of the process.

So let's break this down a bit more.

Use the Product

First, if you want to sell something, you have to be using it. That is an irrefutable, undeniable principle in the universe of sales, direct or otherwise. If you go to the Ford dealership and your salesperson is driving a Chevy from the dealership next door, what are you going to do? Are you going to buy from that person? If you don't believe in the product enough to be using it yourself, how do you think you'll help anyone else believe in the product enough to want to use it? Sales works in one of two ways: either you brainwash and cajole (push, threaten, trick, etc.) a person into making a purchase, or you educate and motivate them into making a purchase. You either force them to buy or you help them to want to buy. Can you guess which method leads to more customer dissatisfaction?

More lawsuits? More returned product? The difference is small on paper but worlds apart in practice.

If you want to be successful you have to use the motivation method. You have to educate your potential customer on the benefits of your product, usually through a demonstration or other product experience, and then let the customer make the leap. You supply the reason to believe, and you let the customer supply the belief. With that in mind, how are you going to convince someone else to believe in something that you don't use yourself and don't believe in yourself? You can't do it. The whole idea behind network marketing is that you're selling a product from which everyone, or nearly everyone can benefit. That's why the word-of-mouth advertising platform becomes so effective, and so necessary. At dōTERRA, for instance, everyone can benefit from the product. If you are still breathing, you can benefit. You may not need to use every product in the line but there is at least one product that would improve your life.

So whatever you're selling, find that selection of products that would improve your own life and start using them. You need to develop the inner conviction that your product is the best on the market and that a person would have to be crazy to not use the product. Until you go that far you won't carry the conviction to convert others. Conviction can't be faked.

In some respects, you can look at this step as identifying the first person you need to sell: yourself. If you can't sell you, whom you know better than anyone else in the world, then you can't expect much success when you try to sell others. Additionally, if you try to sell a product you don't believe in, you're really just trying to con someone. You know the "truth" in the back of your mind — that the product isn't worth buying — yet you're trying to convince someone else to buy it. That's a fundamental violation of integrity and your customers will pick up on your doubts even if they don't consciously know why they're feeling doubtful.

Think about it this way: have you ever tried to tell your friend

* * *

about how awesome a movie was and how your friend should go see it? Have you ever tried to do that about a movie you've never seen? What about one you've never even seen a preview for (because that's a product sample)? You'd be crazy to try to tell your friend about how great a movie was if you hadn't even seen a preview. How would you know what to say? How would you know whether your friend even liked that type of movie? The same thing is true with selling a product or service. You need to have a personal experience with it before you can duplicate that experience for friends, family, and strangers. Start with you. It's the only place you can really start anyway.

Teach Others

Once you believe in the product, then you can begin to tell others about it. That's the way it works, not the other way around. You might learn new things about the product and its effectiveness as you interact with others but your initial belief has to come from a personal experience. Then you can plug into your personal framework the experiences that other people share with you.

Teaching others about the product really stems from your personal belief anyway. Many of the really successful networking professionals I know started out as product evangelists. They had a life-changing experience with a product or service, and then wanted everyone in the world to know about it.

Teaching others to use the product really comes in two phases. The first phase is to open your mouth and familiarize people with the product. The second step is to teach them the finer details and actual usage technique. You can look at this as first establishing the "why" for the product and then teaching the "how" of it. Does that sound familiar?

The world is full of information nowadays. Centuries ago, people learned everything they could just for the sake of learning. They had much more time and availability than they had opportunity. Back then, the typical person learned about as much information in a lifetime as you can find in the weekend edition of your favorite national newspaper today. You could go online right now and learn how to change your oil, fly an airplane, build a tree house, plan a wedding, pan for gold, build a computer, or just about anything else you can think of. The amount of information available to you every day is staggering.

The question, then, is "Why?" Why do you want to learn to change your oil? Fly an airplane? Build a tree house? Maybe some of those things actually interest you but that's because you have a "why" in your head already. Maybe you just hit 5,000 miles and you don't trust the guys at your local auto-service station. Maybe your children have been begging you for a tree house. Maybe your daughter just announced her engagement.

In any case, the "why" preceded the "how," and it always will. We no longer have the time to learn how to do things just because we can. We have to prioritize. We have to decide what's important enough to be worth the time, and what isn't.

So your first step as a networking professional is to give your customer a reason to believe. You have to give that person a convincing, personalized reason to want to learn more. You have to cultivate interest in your potential customer. Developing that curiosity is teaching your customer about the product in the sense that you are opening the customer's eyes to the existence of the product. When I was representing the products of that first networking company, I pushed that water filter technology because people didn't know it existed. It was easy to show it to new prospects and show them the efficacy of the product.

With dōTERRA, it's as simple as getting a few drops of oil into a potential customer's hands. They can take one, deep breathe and feel the immediate clearing effect in their minds. Instantly, they are aware of something that, to them, didn't exist a moment before. That's the first phase of teaching the customer.

But the process doesn't end there. Once the customer is introduced to the product, you have the opportunity to educate.

• • •

Being aware of the product will inspire curiosity, if you have a good product, but that just means more questions to answer. Once you have exposed someone to the product, you need to provide them a means of learning more. You can give them literature, like brochures, books, or Websites; educate them one on one; or invite them to an event. Whatever method you choose to use, just know that you need to provide more information.

Can you imagine seeing the trailer for the best movie you could imagine, and then never being given the chance to see the actual movie? How frustrating would that be? To protect ourselves from a feeling of loss it wouldn't be long before we would start to tell ourselves that the movie couldn't have been that good.

As humans, we tend to do that sort of thing. If we really want something but can't have it, we start to look for reasons to not want it anymore. If you give a potential customer an initial experience with your product but don't follow up and provide a way for the customer to learn more about the product, you are setting that person up for frustration. That frustration will lead to barriers, which will guarantee that you never help them to become a customer or a distributor.

The third and final stage of teaching others about the product is to teach them to follow this same process. Once they have had a personal experience and become converted to the product, you have a customer. At the same time, you have a team member. You have someone who has had a positive product experience and who can now go and share that experience with others, multiplying your efforts.

However, you can't just cut people loose and expect them to build teams of their own. Instead, you need to teach them how to teach others about the product and how to share the product. Once you close that loop, you will grow your team and your business and you will be on the path to success.

After you've done it once, just duplicate the process again and again to climb higher. Continue to use the product and build up your history and experience with the product. Continue to reach out and teach others about the product and how to share it. Duplicate this process again and again, and you'll have success.

Efforts That Can be Duplicated

There's another point I want to make about duplication here. Specifically, what can be duplicated and what cant. I'm speaking in reference to the things that you teach to your team members to help them learn about the product and the business. Certain activities are more easily duplicated than others, and you want to make sure that you're teaching your team members to do things they can do.

For example, I know of a gentleman who has a radio program. He mentions his MLM product frequently in his program, and he has a lot of success with people calling in or visiting his Website to find out more. He's able to enroll a lot of those contacts and as a result, increase his sales. This man has a perfect way to promote his product and introduce customers to something they didn't know about before. He is using the product, and now he's teaching others about it, over and over again. It's network marketing in its simplest form, and he's doing an expert job at it.

So now I should tell everyone else to sign on with a radio network, run their own show, and self-promote, right? No. This is one of those activities that works really well for the few people who have access to it but excludes the vast majority of possible team members. This is a great activity, but it can't be duplicated.

On the other hand, who eats? Everyone eats, right? Who eats out at lunch? If you do, could you find one other person to talk to while you're out? Someone else in the lobby while you're waiting to be seated? The person behind you in line while you're waiting for the cashier to catch up? The same thing holds true with the grocery store, the electronics store, the home improvement store, etc. How often are you ever alone on the bus or train? Make a habit of talking to one other person each day until you've talked to everyone who shares your commute. Then talk to them all again, sharing updates and recent success stories.

You can teach your team how to organize an event at the local recreation center or library, but it'll be harder to teach them how to set up a chiropractic clinic, not to mention the schooling involved. My point is, in your efforts to teach your team about what works in their efforts to prospect, be sure to keep things simple. Teach them how to talk to strangers, family, and friends in the innocuous, random situations they're likely to encounter. Don't focus on the brilliant, unique idea that can't be replicated.

How do you know if something can be duplicated? Look at the simplicity of the task. Talking to someone at the store or the PTA meeting or your other job doesn't take any intensive training or work. Setting up an email blast campaign is a bit more complicated. Co-sponsoring a workout group at the local gym might be way out of a person's league. So, for yourself, use what works. If you have access to a special channel, use it. Sell the product in whatever way works best for you. When it comes to teaching your team, however, teach what can be duplicated. Teach what anybody can use.

Why to Not Frontload

One critical component to building a successful business is to build a broad repeat-customer base. You want a large group of people coming back to you again and again to buy more product. You want results that you can duplicate from month to month so that you can establish consistency in your work and income.

In the process of doing that, make sure you don't try to "frontload." Frontloading is the opposite of duplication, so let me tell you a little about what frontloading is and why it's such a bad thing for your long-term business success. We did a lot of frontloading when I was starting out in network marketing. Frontloading is great for bulking up your paycheck in the short-term. It's kind of like the instant gratification version of network sales, the "get rich quick" version.

The reason behind it is that you get to take a cut of

everything your customer orders. You get a decent percentage of their total purchase price. The obvious equation, then, is to "help" new customers make a large order so that you bring home a piece of that larger order. In a network marketing company where the compensation structure is the competitive advantage — the real product — it can make some sense to frontload, especially if the product itself is lower in quality or less desirable. Zig Ziglar says, "You can only sell an empty box once." What he means is, if your product isn't worth buying, or your potential customer base is small, you almost *need* your customers to place a large order right up front in order for you to get a decent paycheck. But if your product is lackluster, ordinary, useless, or unnecessary, then you are basically selling an empty box. Once the customer buys, that person is going to realize the trap he's fallen into and wish he'd never fallen for your gimmicks in the first place. If that's your game, you need to sell the biggest box you possibly can, because you probably won't get the chance to sell another one.

At dōTERRA our product meets those three, critical criteria for a successful product so there's no need to frontload it. If you need to enroll someone with a single bottle of lemon oil, then do it. Over time, as that person converts more fully to using the products, she will order more and more. However, if you push your customer into frontloading — that is, buying a large quantity of products up front — you won't be able to get another sale next month or the month after, or maybe ever again.

It's hard for customers to justify buying any more product when their garages are already full of inventory that they haven't moved yet. It's also very disheartening for many people when they go out to try to sell and get rejected a few dozen times; that feeling is amplified when the customers remember that their life savings is now tied up in this inventory, and, if they can't sell the product, their retirement is now on the line. When customers end up worried about the future because of the product they've purchased in the past, you run the very real risk of losing them as customers — and they'll usually take their family, friends, and associates down with them.

If you give people a bad experience, they are far more likely to tell anyone and everyone they know about it. If you give people a good experience, they might share with others. (Studies indicate that the unhappy people will speak to six times more people than happy people do.) If you want to come out on top of that balance, you need to be giving far more good experiences than bad ones.

Another reason to avoid frontloading is purely selfish: income stability. If you frontload, you can boost your income for a month, but it comes at the expense of the next month; possibly the next several months. That means next month you'll be looking for another new customer to frontload. And the month after that. And the month after that. And so on.

That gets hard to do after a while because your customers don't advocate for you. They don't go out and tell everyone about how excited they are about this great new product. They're too busy worrying about all the product they now need to sell, and many of them haven't yet developed the skills and the confidence to sell effectively.

When I started out with that first company in the old days, I was instructed to frontload my customers. I had no idea that there might be another way, so I did it. My average initial order size was around $5,000. How many of those customers do you think came back to buy again in month two or three? My income would swing wildly from $25,000 a month to $5,000 a month. There's no stability in that, and the lack of stability stemmed directly from how we were enrolling people with these large orders. I didn't yet understand the principle of having a lot of people order a little product. I was having a few people order a lot of product.

The problem with the frontloading technique is that you are too heavily reliant on any given person. If someone falls through or has a problem that month your income suffers dramatically. By spreading around the same amount of product over a much broader base of customers, you make sure that no single customer has undue influence on your paycheck. You might not get the wild upward swings anymore, but you'll also give up all those tragic downward ones. By having a large number of clients all ordering a small amount of product, you help to level out the "feast or famine" income stream that often comes with network marketing. Instead of living on prime rib one month and ramen noodles the next, you can live reasonably all the time. By enrolling lots of people and letting them make frequent small orders, rather than pushing them to frontload, you can steady your income and have some peace of mind. If a customer suddenly drops out of the program, it won't affect you with the same magnitude as if you're frontloading. There aren't many guarantees in the network marketing profession, but you can help guarantee your own income by making sure your customers feel supported and don't feel pressured. People respond negatively to sales pressure, so you don't want to be the source of that feeling or they will respond negatively to you. It's tough to have success when nobody likes you.

So don't frontload. Instead, follow the higher law of getting small orders from more people. They'll come back to you next month for another order, and you can make a little more then too. That process can be duplicated over and over forever. Frontloading cannot be duplicated so don't rob from tomorrow to live it up today.

5. Get in the Game

"If you always do what you've always done, you'll always get what you've always gotten." —Anonymous

Back when I was working within the business department of a networking company, I went to play basketball and brought my son with me. I mentioned previously1 how he yelled out onto the court for me to "Get off the bench, and get in the game!" Now it's my turn to pass that reminder on to you. Take a look at where you are right now. Are you satisfied with your current employer? Job? Income? Family status? If you are, great. If not, get off the bench, and get in the game.

Now look at where you would be in a perfect world. Have you reached that level in terms of your employer? Your job? Your income? Your family status? If you have, great. If not, get off the bench, and get in the game.

I dare say that very few of us are really fully engaged in the game. We may have some parts of our lives where we're playing with full strength and focus but that often comes without bringing the other aspects of our lives along for the ride. Most of this comes from trying to second-guess whether we're really going in the direction we want to go. Stop trying to second-guess yourself and follow your instincts. Your inner self will guide you to do what you've always dreamed up, if you'll let it. Instead of letting yourself get comfortable with the status quo look for what else you'd like to see in your life. Look for what else you'd like to do with your life, what else you'd like to be. So often, we sit back and wait for life to hand us something only to be disappointed by the nothing we get in return. Life has a way of only giving us what we give it first.

I once heard a metaphor that equated life to an empty box: it's only as good as what you put in it. All that means is that if you want to have an abundant life you need to give abundantly. If you want to have success you need to put in time and effort. If you want kindness you need to put in kindness. I'm not suggesting that life gives back in a one-to-one manner. If that were the case, no one would ever get ahead in life. Thankfully, life returns investments with interest. Unfortunately, that applies to both sides of the coin. If you put in good things, you'll reap good things with interest. If you put in bad things you'll reap compounded misery.

Again, that's not to say that life will turn things around instantly. You generally have to invest a long time before you start to see the real rewards – like our penny example. Over the short-term, life will continue to have its ups and downs. The question is whether your ups and downs, on the average, are higher or lower than they were before. If you want your ups and downs to move in an upward direction over time, you need to "get off the bench, and get in the game."

The Right Person

It's interesting to me, in hindsight, that I did what I did when I went to interview with those ladies and joined the first network marketing company. I'm not surprised that I tried out what they said, but I am stunned that I was able to take what they taught me, teach myself some more, and find success. I don't think anyone ever would have guessed that I was going to make something out of that opportunity. I certainly didn't have the appearance or background to indicate to anyone that I was the "right" person to enjoy that level of success.

People frequently ask me, "How do I find the 'right' person?" or "How do I find that person who will really launch my business?" I get that question — sometimes actually used as an excuse — a lot nowadays.

The answer is, "You don't." Don't judge. That's not your place. You actually don't care who you're bringing on as long as those people are honest. You obviously don't want to bring a bunch of crooks on board. That would be bad for your credibility, bad for your business, and bad for your future as a free citizen of this country. I am eternally grateful that there were no pictures taken the day I met with those ladies in downtown Logan, Utah. Why? Let me paint the picture for you of who they saw walking into their office to learn about a job opportunity.

I was only 22 years old at the time, not the established, successful future team member they could have hoped for. To top it off, I have a distinct memory of what I was wearing. I was dressed in khakis, cowboy boots, and purple suspenders. That's right. Cowboy boots and suspenders. *Purple* suspenders.

I can pretty much guarantee that those women didn't go home that night talking to each other about how they'd just found "the guy" who was going to really go through with the program. They weren't breaking out in song and dance in celebration of my arrival. They were probably doing just the opposite. They probably went home that night and cried together. "We spent that money and put that ad in the paper, and *this* is what came in? What are we going to do now?" Still, I showed up, so they gave me a chance. You can bet that they were thrilled about that little gamble.

You never know who your big leaders are going to be. Most people won't bite that hard. Most people won't want to get involved in the business; they'll just want to use the product. That's fine. You need customers. Of the few who do bite, most will just be little fish. They've got other things going on and this business isn't going to replace their full-time job (even though it could). Does that mean you don't bother getting people enrolled? Absolutely not. My answer is to enroll anyone and everyone you can. Let *them* make the decision about whether they are going to be a customer, small fish, or whale shark. If you don't make the offer, however, you'll never get any of those master builders on your team.

Do "perfect" networking professionals exist? Sure. Every once in a while someone will enroll a person who just explodes out the gate. There are people out there who are ready and waiting for the right opportunity and just don't know it yet. Given the right opportunity they'll blow your business out of the water and all you have to do is get out of the way. That's a rare situation. It's the exception, not the rule. In general, you have to cultivate your leaders. You have to plant the seed and then tend to it, nurture it, and help it grow. Then, in time, those people will become the amazing leaders you've always wanted and everyone else will ask you how you found them. The answer is that you didn't find them, you grew them.

Even though I didn't turn around and make a million dollars in my second week, I turned out pretty well eventually. Remember, my first event on my own was a complete bust. How do you explain that one if I'm supposed to be the "right" guy? The truth is that I'm not the "right" guy or at least I wasn't. I had to learn and grow and develop just the same as anyone else.

My recommendation, therefore, is to stop judging. You don't know what's going on between a person's ears. So what if he showed up wearing cowboy boots and purple suspenders? Give him a chance and see what happens. At dōTERRA everyone needs our product. If they are on this side of the dirt, if they can still fog a mirror, they qualify. Anyone who needs the product can also benefit from the business, although not everyone will.

I have a friend, for example, who has an insurance practice. He makes several hundred thousand dollars a year with his insurance company. Could he make more by joining my business? Who knows? Probably. That doesn't matter though. For him, there's no pain there. He doesn't feel a need to get into another business enterprise but he orders from me every month. He loves the product and will remain a customer forever; but he doesn't care about the business side of things.

When you talk to people, educate them on the product and then inform them about the potential of the business. Get them enrolled in the program and then let them make their own decisions. Sometimes, your best business partners will actually be the people who adamantly refuse to be part of the business. I have one lady in particular who is the most amazing product evangelist. She is so passionate about the product that she ends up enrolling seven or eight people a month. Conventional wisdom says that enrolling two people a month is good, so seven or eight is obviously fantastic. But she refuses to "do the business." I look at her, and do you know what my response is? "Great. You just keep on *not* doing the business." Why? Because she's actually doing the business and the last thing I want is to wake her up to that and somehow adversely impact her drive to share the product. I don't want to take her focus from her by pointing out that she's doing the business already and doing it better than a lot of other people. I want her to just keep on doing what she's doing.

Is she one of the "right" people? I don't even think about it that way anymore. I just think about whether she's in a position to be helped by the product and then be helped by the business. If the answers to those two questions are "yes," then she's the "right" person —whether she accepts that or not.

Becoming the Right Person

My advice is to stop looking for the "right" person and start developing the ones you already have. Your best leaders won't walk in with the full, polished skill set. They'll develop that skill set over time. Why? Because if someone walks in with the full skill set, they also walk in with limited desire for self-improvement. Even when someone walks in weak and behind, that person has an incentive to learn and grow and become more. Those people tend to keep learning and growing long after they've reached that "right person" plateau — often passing by the "right" people on the path upward. Whether a person is right for the business is more a question of whether they're willing to learn and grow on their own time and less a question of what skills and knowledge they already have. The networking profession is rooted in self-improvement and self-motivation. If you have those two things, you can be successful.

As in any career or sport, if you come in with all the skills and none of the drive your career will probably resemble a firework. You'll shoot up, explode, and then fizzle out. Unless you are willing to keep pushing yourself the end is a question of "when," not "if."

The right person wants to keep learning. The right person isn't content to sit still or be complacent or relax and draw down on a residual income. The right person is the one that keeps trying, again and again, no matter how seemingly small the results may be. So stop looking and start developing. The right people are all around you; you just need to help them uncover their potential. That's your job. The vast majority of the people you encounter — including many of those who seem like the "right" people — are comfortable being comfortable. They are either unwilling to try something new, like the networking profession, or they are unwilling to stretch themselves to reach for big successes. Some just simply don't see the potential of the business.

Many of these people have all the talents to thrive in the business but they just don't care about making that kind of effort. They're happy (complacent) where they are. There's no immediate pain in their current situation, so there's no drive to change the situation. After all, in order to achieve success by harnessing potential outside what you've already harnessed, you must step outside your comfort zone and do something that stretches you. You have to try something new, to push a little harder, try a new approach. Doing so is often uncomfortable, by definition, and most people don't want to go there.

Take the most basic part of the networking profession as an example: you have to talk to people. You can start out by talking to your family and friends, of course, but you'll eventually run out of those—and, for some people, talking to family and friends can actually be harder than talking to strangers. Either way eventually you'll have to start talking to people you don't know. That's really hard for many people. We get so caught up in our routines that we have a difficult time breaking them. We go to the grocery store and shop in silence rather than talking to that other person in the aisle with us. Half the time, we don't even talk to the cashier beyond the cursory "How's it going?"

Breaking out of that habit is uncomfortable. It requires us to violate not only our own comfort zone but also another's comfort zone. That's a double whammy, and it's hard to do. Thankfully it gets easier with practice. Otherwise, for people who can't break through that discomfort barrier, they put a lid on their growth. They can only go so far before they are capped and stopped.

The comfort zone itself is like a giant, protective dome around you, which can seem really nice. The problem is that it protects indiscriminately. It will protect you from some bad things but it will also protect you from good things. The only way to break through that glass ceiling and move forward is to go to the edge of your comfort zone and then take another step. Interestingly, your comfort zone won't trap you inside and it will usually grow to surround you again once you step out of it. In addition it will continue to grow as long as you keep trying to walk out of it.

That said, stepping through that barrier isn't easy at first, but you have to do it if you want to have success in a networking profession. That's the only way to really network. You need to meet new people and then get them to try your product. From there, it's just a matter of educating the customer, and they'll buy.

When we find something great it's human nature to tell our friends and family. When we find something awful, we tell our friends and family. Think about the last movie you saw in the theater. Did you like it? Was it awful? Who did you talk to about it afterward? The same thing holds true with everything else in society. Social media gains its strength from this inner drive to share experiences, thoughts, and impressions. If you can get your product into a customer's hands and give that customer a good experience with it, the person is sure to tell other people about it.

The Wrong People

Now, while you may not always be able to pick out the "right" people, you can certainly pick out the wrong people. The wrong people aren't wrong in the sense that they'll never take off and build your business for you — though that's often true as well. The wrong people are the ones who become a distraction or a drag on your progress. These are the people you spend far too much time on in relation to the success they bring.

Again, they aren't wrong to have in your organization. They're just wrong to spend all your time on. As I've said before, only about half of the people you ever meet will be wired to really understand the business side of things. In the Western Hemisphere, only 50 percent of the population is cognitively hard-wired to function as a self-employed entrepreneur. In other words, half of all of our prospects aren't equipped with the inner motivation and guidance necessary to take off and run on their own. Again, most of these people will be end users of your products instead, and that's a good thing too. If you want a successful organization, however, you need a lot of people who will order a little product each month. That's how you have success. So don't ignore people just because they aren't wired to become your next builder. Be aware of their level of understanding and support them accordingly. These people become the "wrong" people when we start spending a disproportionate amount of time trying to get them to the next level.

I had an experience once where I was sharing product with a woman who had rheumatoid arthritis. For background's sake, rheumatoid arthritis is basically chronic inflammation in the joints, and it can be both painful and crippling. There are a number of different medications out there to treat the condition and this woman was on several, as well as several more medications to treat the side effects of the medication. I recognized her need and showed her a combination of oils and other products that could support her healing process. She liked what she saw. Then I informed her of the price tag. For about $75 a month she could be symptom-free (because it's an auto-immune disease, there isn't a real "cure"). Judging from the number of medications she was taking, she was spending at least $250 a month on medicine — medicines she could possibly wean herself off of by switching to the oils. She wouldn't do it. She was so fixated on the $75 per month (which is a significant amount) that she couldn't convince herself to do it, even though it could have saved her the $250 per month. She would have increased her net, available cash each month by $175 but she couldn't see it. She couldn't connect those dots.

It's very easy to spend too much time trying to convince people like that of the error of their thinking, but you'd just be wasting your time. Half of the people you meet, regardless of intelligence, just won't be able to grasp the concepts. I had a friend on my team who was an example of this to me. He happened to be in an area which was just opening up to the network marketing company we were working in, and people were enrolling right and left. He landed in the middle of that and through no real effort on his part ended up with a fairly strong business team. He should have been making a pretty decent commission each month but he wasn't placing his own order. He wasn't buying any product so he was disqualifying himself from what his organization had earned. The sad thing was that he could have bought the minimum order and put it directly in the garbage can without suffering a loss because he was making more than that through his network. His commission would have more than compensated him for the product he threw away.

I talked to him about it again and again, month after month. I tried to explain that he was leaving money on the table but he was still fixated on the cost of that monthly order. He didn't want to spend any money to make his money, so he didn't make anything. Finally, knowing approximately what his checks would be, I offered to place an order on his behalf in exchange for his commission check. I placed the order but I never got that commission check. After that, however, my friend never missed making his monthly order again. When he got that check, it was enough to wrap his brain around what I'd been trying to explain to him for months.

I just hate to look back on all that time I spent trying to explain it to him when what I really needed to do was show him. Still, I wish my friend's experience was the case more often. In my experience, some people won't make that connection even when they see the check in the mail. For those people, the only option left is to just say "next" and move on.

For the people who aren't wired to be entrepreneurs, they can still contribute to your organization. The challenge is that you'll need to instruct them on what to do and how to do it. They can be brilliant, effective people, but they'll need specific instructions. They are waiting to be told what to do, so tell them.

So again, the best course of action is to invite everyone and then offer support based on their interest. If you aren't trying to push them, the entrepreneurs will emerge and become self-starters, others will follow along (as they are looking for a leader to follow), and still others will drop off. You just need to forge on ahead and lead the way. As the saying goes, "You can't push a rope."

Three Needs of New Team Members

Our company is only about six years old, and we've already got people out-earning us, although we were there from the very beginning. I fully believe that in ten years when you look at our top producers you'll see most of the names that are there today. I also think there will be a number of names, quite a few of them, of people who aren't even enrolled yet.

We're six years in, but we're still just getting started. We're not selling in a mature market, so there's a lot of space for upward growth and we have yet to find all the people who will, one day, be our top distributors. Most of them are still out there waiting to be found. The catch is, many of them aren't going to look like top distributors in the same way that I didn't look like a top builder of that first network marketing company when I showed up for my interview in purple suspenders! Don't try to guess who is going to grow your business and who is going to just tread water. Give everyone a chance, and let them sink or swim as they will.

That said, obviously, you want people to swim. You want them to succeed, even if it means they outpace you because network marketing is all about getting a little piece of the efforts of many people, so you want many successful people on your team in order to take a little piece of everything they're creating

With that in mind, I'd like to tell you about the three things every new team member needs in order to get them in the game. Conveniently, this is also what you need to get back in the game if you've strayed. By helping your team members find these three things, you'll be greatly increasing the likelihood that they will catch the vision instead of giving up before they reach the end of the proverbial month with their doubling penny.

The three things are:
1. Information
2. Progress
3. Profits

Why these three things and why are they in this order? Because each element builds on the previous one to lift up that team member. Each one contributes to the foundation upon which the next element can build in logical progression.

Information

Information comes first because information serves as the basis for everything else. It becomes the foundation upon which a person can build. And, it doesn't require a lot of new information to start the ball rolling. Getting even just a little information will boost confidence, which will drive actions. As you learn a little, you can act on that new knowledge. Then, as you learn more you can act on that additional information, building over time as you learn new things, putting them into practice.

One caution here is that it's easy to go to the extreme on information. Very few people will attempt to go out and sell with no knowledge or information. No matter how confident a person is with sales in general, hardly anybody would try to sell a product with no idea of what the product is. The extreme I see more often is in the people who feel the need to learn everything before they'll open their mouths at all. This is bad for many reasons. Two of the main reasons are: 1) the time lost in the learning phase, and 2) the perception a person like this gives off.

In the essential oils world, we have pages and pages of information including books, journals, research studies, anecdotes, brochures, product instruction labels, and more. To attempt to learn all that there is to know would be overwhelming. What's more, we're constantly learning new things: new applications, new combinations, and new deliveries. For a person to say that he wants to know everything before beginning to sell is the same as that person saying he isn't ever going to begin selling, period. There's just too much information out there to digest as a prerequisite for selling. You would lose years of your life — treating your study of oils as a full-time job or an advanced degree — before you ever felt ready to go out and share the product. That's years of time when you could have been sharing and growing your business.

You don't need to know upper-level calculus to help your child with his elementary-school-level math homework. You can do addition and subtraction without understanding integrals and derivatives. The same holds true with network marketing. You can sell, starting right away, based on the information you already know, especially if the product has the three essential traits. Waiting until you know everything is just a waste of time.

Will you meet people who have questions you don't know the answer to if you start now? Absolutely. But you'll also find many people who are ready to involve themselves based on just the information you currently have, with the promise of more information in the future.

Secondly, if you really did know everything there was to know, there's a good chance that you would just frustrate people. When we interact with others, we want to believe that they know what they're talking about. At the same time, however, we want to know that they're still human. If you really did know everything there was to know about essential oils, potential customers would expect you to be at the head of the company, not starting out. Because you spent all your time researching rather than building you won't be at the head of anything. That triggers a warning in people's minds. People don't like to be talked to by fanatics unless the prospect is also fanatical about the very same thing.

If you're crazy about a sports team, other diehard fans will talk to you all day but people who don't follow your sport won't be as interested in talking to you. The problem with limiting yourself to other diehard fans in network marketing is that they are already involved and you can't grow your own business that way.

It's still fun to rub shoulders with people who share common interests but you won't experience progress that way.

Progress

The second need every new team member experiences is progress. Whenever you start something new in life, you want to be able to see and measure the progress you make along the way. That's just human nature. It's also the reason that so many people give up their New Year's resolutions before they hit the second month of the year.

When you start out with a new fitness goal, it's hard to see those results in the first few weeks, much less days or minutes, so it can be very disheartening to stick with the goal. We have this perception in our heads that after working out for two weeks that the workout should become easy. Unfortunately, the nature of working out effectively means it'll never be easy. That would defeat the purpose of working out.

Still, it can be depressing to see no progress and improvement. The same could be said for creating a long report at work. A short memo comes together fairly quickly, and then you have the final product. You can go from start to finish so quickly that you complete the task before you get bored. A long report is a different story, however. You might spend days or weeks just gathering all the preliminary material before you ever spend a second working on the final product. Then, once you do start working on the report, you could easily put hours and hours into the project before anything identifiable really comes together. The advantage in the work situation is that you're probably getting paid to write the report, so there's at least some incentive to continue.

The fact remains that our world wants to see the results *yesterday* for the effort we put in today. We want the reward before we do the work. That's why we have so much consumer debt. People are calculating the payments and saying they can buy today and pay it off with work they do tomorrow. Seeing progress is a tall hurdle to clear so it's critical that people see it in their new business venture, or they'll give up. The scary thing is that you might only have a couple weeks to help your new team member experience that progress or he might be tempted to drop out and look for something with faster results. Thankfully, progress doesn't necessarily mean that your new team member needs to end up in the interstellar-diamond-emperor club either. It can be as simple as getting someone else to come to an event or talking to a stranger and having that person be interested.

The best way for someone to see progress in their business is by focusing on what I call "rain-maker" activities, or those activities that actually build your business. Inviting, sharing, sampling and following-up! The idea here is that everyone needs to see, within the first couple of weeks to a month, some sign that there's a chance for success. They need to get someone to an event or make a small sale or stir up some genuine interest in prospective customers. If a new team member can experience things like that — and string together enough experiences to keep going — the success will eventually come and that team member will stick with the program.

If the progress doesn't show quickly enough it won't be there to fill in when the new team member eventually loses that euphoric, narcotic effect that stems from trying something exciting and new.

• • •

At that point, your new partner will be in very serious risk of moving on and you'll lose the chance to help him see profits.

Profit

The third thing that people need to see stems directly from progress and is the most common indicator for success that euphoric, narcotic matter how much time we might free up or how much stress we might alleviate by going into business for ourselves, none of us would ever stick it out indefinitely if there was no income involved.

At some point, we've got bills to pay and food to buy. Without some profit we're unlikely to stay with a venture for long.

Profits are, deep down, the reason people begin a business endeavor in network marketing. Happily the idea of income supplementation often turns into income replacement. We all have this hope, somewhere inside, that we really can start a business on our own — that we really can be successful all on our own merits and not because we schmoozed the boss better than the next person.

The reason profits become the most common measuring rod for success is because it puts everything onto a common scale. If you made $100 and I made $10, we can agree that you made more. If it took you 20 hours and only took me one hour, we can agree that I was more efficient. There's little need for debate or interpretation about efficiency, effectiveness or success. It's easy to see and compare the results.

Additionally, almost everything in life today takes money – you even have to pay money just for earning money (taxes). For that reason, income and profits are an integral part of our lives. Thankfully, when it comes to network marketing, profits don't have to start out very big. In fact, my experience has taught me that the amount of money you make on your first check is actually irrelevant. The timing, preferably in that first few weeks (a month at most), is far more important than the amount.

I get some disagreement here because some people believe

that a bigger check is better. On the one hand, I agree. On the other hand, they're arguing a different point altogether. I'm saying that you need to see results — profit — within the first few weeks in order to confirm to yourself that the system works. The amount of profit for that confirmation doesn't matter. What matters is that you tried something new, and it paid out a return. That will build your confidence in your ability and in the system, making you more likely to go out there and do it again in order to get a bigger check the next time.

That said, getting a big first check isn't a bad thing. I think my first check was something like $14. Would I have been happier with $140, $1,400, or even $14,000? Maybe. Who knows? What mattered was that I tried the process and it worked. Once I knew that, I knew I just needed to keep following the process if I wanted to move from $14 to $140 and onward, so I did.

Still, the size of that first check can cause some disappointment if it's too small. When that happens, however, it's up to you to reach out to that team member and reassure him or her. Remind the person that any check at all means the system works, and now it's time to keep pushing, building that momentum into something unstoppable. Over time, small efforts can compound into great things. The size of the first check is just the size of the first step, but the size of the first step has no bearing on the size of the next, the next, or the next.

Confidence Breeds Success

Help your new team members meet these three needs in the first month or so and you'll have set the hook. They won't be perfect, and they won't be top producers yet, but they'll be on their way. Just make sure you continue to support and train them over time so that they don't get complacent later.

By helping your new team members meet these three needs you'll be building their confidence, and confidence breeds success. In other words, you'll be setting up your team members to enjoy success now and in the future as long as they continue to follow through.

Interestingly, when I teach classes about this I often ask the question, "If you were making $10,000 per month from your efforts with this company, would you have the confidence to go and talk to anyone else in this room?" People feel like they would have all the confidence in the world to go and talk to anyone else about anything else if they were just making enough money first. Somehow, they think that confidence is tied back into how much money they make. Now, I'm not sure why $10,000 per month is such a magic number, but it is. People come back to it again and again. They seem to feel like someone has "made it" when that person's income reaches that level. I'm not sure why, because that's actually not that high of a number, but the effect is there anyway.

If you want to make more money — at least in the networking profession — you need to have confidence first. As you focus on yourself and what you and your product have to offer, you can sell to others and then teach them to do the same. As your confidence in the process grows you will have success. As your success grows, your confidence in yourself will grow with it, and the process will continue to spiral upward.

The problem is, success will rarely grow on its own. Success has to be dragged out and pulled up by confidence, so you can't wait for success to build the confidence or you'll never get there. Instead, you need to focus on building the confidence and then the success (paycheck) will follow. We build that confidence by supplying a little information, testing the information to see if it moves us forward, then seeing the profits from that forward progress. The system is simple to follow, and it works. Best of all, the confidence doesn't necessarily have to be confidence in yourself. You don't necessarily need to magically shed all your insecurities overnight before you can have success. You can have confidence in the product or confidence in the process even if you don't yet have self-confidence. Confidence in the company counts too because it'll give you confidence that you'll have the support you need.

As your confidence grows in all the related aspects of your business, your confidence in yourself will grow too. You'll start to realize that you really can have success based on your own efforts, and that will give you the confidence that others can have the same success. Once you're sure that others can win alongside you, you'll be more confident in going out to talk to people about joining your team and more confident about training them through the same process.

So, the take away here is that we need to work on our confidence first by following this simple process, and the compensation will take care of itself over time. Anyone can do that. It's simple, so stop trying to second-guess people and just get everyone involved. Get yourself in the game, then get everyone else there too.

6. Master Your Universe

"Whether you think you can or you can't, either way, you are right."
—Henry Ford

If you take a quarter outside at night and hold it up against the night sky, are you covering very much area? No. Not really. About a square inch is all, right?

What you may or may not know is that behind that quarter you're holding up are countless numbers of little twinkling lights that your eye isn't even sophisticated enough to see. It may not look like you're covering up all that much until you attach the Hubble Space Telescope to your eye and look again. Suddenly you'll see thousands of tiny points of light. Stars you never knew existed, right? Wrong. Those aren't stars. They're galaxies. Collections of thousands and millions and billions and *trillions* of stars.

Behind that one quarter you're holding, there are more stars than you could count in an entire lifetime. If you were to count one star per second from the moment you were born until the moment you died about 70 or 80 years later — without ever stopping to eat or sleep — you could only count a small fraction of the stars up there behind that quarter.

Feeling small yet? Do you really want to be in charge of everything?

In the words of the philosopher Alan C. Watts, "Man is a little germ, that lives on an unimportant rock ball, that revolves about an insignificant star on the outer edges of one of the smaller galaxies." That's us.

The only significant characteristic of our sun is that it's not too hot or too cold. Even our planet is remarkably insignificant except for its apparent youth. The heavy metals we have on earth (gold, silver, lead, uranium, etc.) were formed in the hearts of massive stars elsewhere in the cosmos billions of years ago.

You can look at that as the most amazing coincidence of

● ● ●

serendipity ever, or as an act of God, as I do. Either way, as Mr. Watts continues, "But on the other hand, if you think about that for a few minutes I am absolutely amazed to discover myself on this rock ball." I too am amazed and humbled when I realize how small we are and how extraordinary it is that we exist at all. In the words of Peter Falk from the movie "Faraway, So Close," "Life is an exceptional situation."

Why do I go on about this? Because too often we get it into our heads that we somehow run the show. The truth is, the president of the United States can't even run the country alone; how do you think you are going to run the universe alone? I might recommend, in fact, that you start carrying a quarter around with you just to remind you of how big the universe is. Why? Because you need to resign daily from your position as the General Manager of the Universe. There is so much that goes on in life over which you have no control at all. Zero. Zilch. Nada. Nothing. You need to resign that position as GM of the universe so that you can focus on what's closer to home, on the things you *can* control.

You need to look up at the heavens, recognize that you can't run everything, and then do everything you can to run what you can. Focus on what's close to home. You can't control the weather, but you don't have to let it control you either. You can't control other people — even family members (especially family members!) — but you can control how you interact with them.

The idea here is to focus on what you can control and build your own universe around those things. Build your universe, your center, around the things you can control and then become the master of that universe.

Building Your Universe

The first thing to do is figure out what you have control over and what you don't. The simple answer to that question is that you have control over yourself, your feelings, and your actions. And that's it. You don't have control over your children, spouse, siblings, parents, neighbors, or the strangers around you. Some would argue that thought but the truth is that you only have control over yourself. You can't *make* your children do anything, for instance. If your child doesn't want to brush his or her teeth, you can't make that child do it. You can take control of your own actions and brush the child's teeth, or you can control your actions to apply coercive pressure on the child, but you can't mind-control your children and force them to do anything. Those of you with children understand this concept all too well.

So, if the only thing you can control is you, does that mean that you should build your universe around yourself, that you should become your own world and ignore everyone and everything else? No. What you should do is build your universe around where you (and what you can control) interact with the outside world, family, friends, etc. If you pull your focus in too tightly, you won't be able to see where to move. You'll have not only put on blinders, you'll have flipped them closed over your eyes. How will you know what actions to take in that circumstance?

If you don't focus at all, however, you'll be distracted by everything else going on around you and you'll end up spending far too much effort trying to change or direct things over which you have no control — things outside your personal universe. We'll talk more about distraction in a few chapters however, so we won't get distracted by that here.

In your universe, you should include everything over which you have control: yourself, your feelings, and your actions. You should also include what you can influence: how your actions can encourage others to make actions favorable to you. Then, especially when you're seeking business success, you need to put your blinders on, ignore the galaxies behind that quarter, and focus on what you can control that will bring results. In other words, focus on the business. You have complete control over your productivity, your ordering, and your personal development.

First, concentrate on your productivity. You have complete

control, for example, over how many events you organize. You have control over what types of events you organize and what topics are covered. If you choose to be the speaker, you have control over what is said. If you call in a guest speaker or another expert you are giving up control over exactly what's said and retaining control only over what topic is assigned. Your speaker then has control over whether or not that topic is actually covered.

You also have complete control over how many phone calls you make, how many thank-you cards you send, how many follow-up emails you transmit, and how many new people you talk to. If you don't open your mouth, who else can make you do that? No one.

Your universe includes how many samples you give out and how many product guides you pass along. You get to choose whether or not you do the vital behaviors. No one else can make that decision for you, and you can't make that decision for anyone else. You can't master their universe; you can only master your own.

Second, you also have complete control over your own ordering. Most companies will have a discount program or other incentive for consistent monthly ordering but the decision of how much and when you order is still yours and yours alone. Take advantage of those programs when you can because they'll help you accelerate your progress; but remember that your order is yours to control.

Your upline leader can't control your order any more than you can control how much your team orders. Everyone gets to make that decision on her own terms, and it's up to you to maximize that aspect of your business. It's up to you to order what you need so that you have it on hand for when you need it. If your stock is getting low, place an order. It's that simple. If you don't take control of that aspect of your business, you won't be able to create the success you want.

Third, you have complete control over how much personal development you do — or don't do. No one can force you to learn and grow any more than you can force someone else to learn or grow. And can I tell you a secret? Network marketing is, in many respects, the profession of personal development. The people who achieve high levels of lasting, real success in the networking profession do so because they really focus on that inner core of their personal universe: themselves. Your productivity and your ordering are in your universe — you have total control over those things — and your interactions with others, but none of those things are the core. The core of your universe — your personal star — is what you do to develop and improve yourself.

Personal Development

So what is personal development? Simply put, personal development is the mechanism by which you keep yourself on track, up to date, and ready for anything. Eric Hoffer once said, "In times of change, learners inherit the earth, while the learned find themselves beautifully equipped to deal with a world that no longer exists."

There is a saying that goes, "All organizations are perfectly designed to get the results they get." I would assert that people are too. In other words, if you are dissatisfied with your current level of success, you need to change yourself so that you can produce better results. The vital behaviors are simple, and you can duplicate them all day long, but you'll still be limited at a "glass ceiling." This is the idea that there is a level to which you will rise before going no higher – a cap or lid on your progress. We all have a glass ceiling. We can *see* further but we can't *get* any further. The reason we can't get further is because we aren't equipped to do so. Once you have undergone the necessary developmental changes, you will be able to reach that new level.

That's why daily personal development is so critical in network marketing. In the "real world" people are limited by their organizations long before they are limited by themselves. In network marketing, the organization is flexible enough to enable to you grow just as quickly as you want, so there's no reason to throttle yourself back by neglecting your personal development.

Conveniently, opportunities for personal development are all around. You can attend workshops, product demonstrations, book clubs, or college classes. You can host events, attend events, sample new products, read about new products, or talk to others about new products.

For me, one of the simplest ways to develop a habit of personal development is to read just 10 pages of a good book every day. I got this idea from Jeff Olsen, author of "Slight Edge" (we'll be talking more about him in the final chapter), and it's worked wonders in my life. Reading just 10 pages doesn't take very long in any given day, but do the math over the course of a year: that's 3,650 pages. That's a dozen or more books over the course of this year — and each and every year of your life still to come. Don't feel like you have time to read the books? Thankfully, many of them are available in audio format, so you can just listen to them instead. The audio versions enable you to take advantage of that otherwise lost time during your commute. Instead of listening to music or talk radio all the time you can attend a little Drive-Time University.

Now, when I say "good" books, I don't mean the latest bestselling thriller or teen romance or fantasy blockbuster. I don't even mean high-minded literary fiction and I certainly don't mean cheap, straight-to-paperback romances and cowboy novels. You're welcome to read those kinds of books — especially if you're reading them in place of sitting in front of the broke box — but you won't find much self-improvement tucked in the pages of the latest science fiction mystery. You can choose to read whatever you want, but I would recommend that you read books that teach you something new, not just books that entertain. This book is, for example, a self-development book. I'm teaching you concepts and principles you can use to improve yourself. There are hundreds, if not thousands of "good books" available, and more are being published every day. Pick one and start reading. As you do, you'll find your mind opening to its inner workings, and you'll gain a better appreciation for how

• • •

you and others tick. You can also learn new skills and techniques to apply in your business and advance your success. Of course, you'll never be able to absorb everything you read. There's just too much information out there. The good news is that you don't need to absorb it all. Just fill your cup to full with good, actionable, quality information and be content with that.

One of the things I do is to read with the intent to teach others. When I read, I'm looking for the bits and pieces that I can apply, the pieces I can turn around and teach. I do this for two reasons: first, you'll never make it through all the personal-development material out there; and second, the best way to learn is to teach someone else what you have discovered.

There is a wealth of material out there — good material — and more coming every day as research is translated into actionable information. You'll never have time to get through it all. Don't try. Don't worry about it. Absorb what you can and keep moving forward. I recommend that you focus on less. Meaning, identify the dozen or so books that will change your life forever, and master those, reading them over and over again. Study them. This is better than having an entire library of self-help books that you have never read or maybe read quickly once. While reading, envision a specific person (or group of people) whom you could teach, a significant other, a child, a colleague, or a stranger. Once you have that person in mind, pretend that you are preparing a lesson to share with him or her. This technique is actually supported by all kinds of research.

When you approach a topic in this way, you'll naturally look at it differently. You'll look at it from multiple angles, trying to anticipate and then answer possible questions and issues. You'll commit things to memory rather than letting them go in your eyes and out the back of your head. Then, even better than just reading with a mindset of preparation, actually go out and share the concepts and principles. Go and teach that someone whatever it was that you prepared. In doing so, you'll reinforce the material in your own mind and give an opportunity to that other person to be exposed to something he or she might not have otherwise encountered.

I do this by preparing brief thoughts for my conference calls. I'm on a conference call almost every day, and I like to set the tone by sharing some tidbit of wisdom. Those tidbits typically come from whatever I'm reading at the time. I like to expose my team members to the information so that they can learn and grow from it. I like to push them to think about something new and different in order to stretch their comfort zones. In the words of Emerson, "Unless you try to do something beyond what you have already mastered, you will never grow."

In network marketing, your personal growth and development is key to your business growth and development, meaning your success. If you don't take the time to improve yourself, you'll be that much less likely and less equipped to improve your business — and that means that much less success in the end. A warning! If you ever think you are done learning, you are done! Learning and self-development are a never-ending quest.

Pay Yourself

One of the other things you do to improve yourself is to learn control and restraint. For about the last two and a half years Keri and I have not taken a pay raise. We have paid ourselves the same stipend each month out of our paycheck even though the check itself has grown over that time. We've done that partly to maintain our financial discipline. We want to make sure that we can live on much less than we make, so we mapped out our budget of what we need as a family, and we take that as our portion of the paycheck each month. When we start to push on the boundary of that reduced paycheck, we start looking for ways to minimize our family expenses.

The other reason we don't take our whole check each month is because the business requires significant re-investment. Like any business, network marketing or otherwise, my business at dōTERRA requires us to re-invest capital. We have employees to pay, marketing and advertising expenses, travel expenses like you wouldn't believe, event and seminar costs and product expenses. We give out limited quantities of product as samples to prospective customers. All of that is an expense to our business. By re-investing in our business, we are actually paying ourselves. We're using our money to make more money, continuing to accelerate that process and set up that engine.

I see a lot of distributors come online without that understanding: the realization that they need to re-invest to grow their business. For many people, it's because they start out as hobbyists. They aren't really in it for the business; they're in it for the product. That's fine. In the beginning, as a hobbyist, you may not need to re-invest much. If you got started just to get the discount on product you may not need to re-invest at all. But once you get serious about the business, you need to get serious about the business. You need to ask yourself: am I running this like a business or as a hobby?

Every major company out there re-invests a portion of its earnings. In order to grow, a company needs to be able to spend money. That money has to come from somewhere. It can either take out a loan and end up paying interest, or it can take a loan from itself by re-investing profits. There are pluses and minuses to both funding methods, but you'll need to put money back into your business if you want it to be a true business.

If you went to the grocery store and there was nothing on the shelves, would you spend any money there? Of course not. How about if the lights were turned off or if the paint on the walls was peeling? The same will be true for you. If you don't have product to sell, how can your customers ever buy from you? People like to have the product the moment that they buy it. For subsequent purchases, they may be willing to just place an order but you'll still want product on hand for new customers and for "emergency" purchases.

One of the other uses for that inventory is as samples for your potential customers. I'm not sure how samples are given out in a service-based company, but in a product-based organization you should be giving a small sample to potential customers. The idea behind this is simple: you want the customer to have a personal experience so that the customer can convert to the use of the product or service.

Another great use for product inventory is promotions. People generally are incentive- minded, meaning they are asking themselves, "What's in it for me if I enroll now?" It is appropriate at times (but not all the time) to offer an added bonus of a free product or two to incentivize the right behavior. To have those samples or promotions available you're going to have to invest your own money into the business.

This isn't the same as just giving away money because your product, not your giveaways, should bring the customer back to you. After sampling your product the customer will hopefully come back and buy more. When they do, you'll recoup your investment and more. That's how you invest in your business. It's also how you convert people into product evangelists so that they, eventually, become members of your team.

You'll also invest in your business by advertising. Advertising will take the form of handouts, brochures, and third-party materials. You'll also be spending time letting people know about upcoming events and then possibly buying a small gift of appreciation for your guest speakers.

Travel is one of my biggest expenses. It won't start out that way for you, but it may end up that way over time. I expense my mileage and airfare for traveling to events, my hotel room when I stay somewhere, and even meals in some circumstances. I'm not trying to step in and advise you on tax deductions or anything else at this point; you should consult a CPA for that. I'm just trying to point out that it's expensive to run a business, and that money has to come from somewhere.

If you want to be successful in the network marketing profession, you can't just look at it as a hobby. It has to be a real career for you or it will never take off and reach its true potential. If you treat it like a hobby it will remain a hobby and in general, hobbies cost money, they don't make money. The key here is to make a conscious decision about whether you just want to be a hobbyist or if you want to run a legitimate business that can make you money. If you don't want to grow your hobby into a full-fledged business, then don't. If you want to replace any other income with the greatest form of residual income, then you will need to treat your business as a business. You can only reap what you sow.

A Common Difficulty

I also want to take this opportunity to warn you about a situation I see over and over again with incoming distributors. So many people have difficulty making that initial transition from hobby to business in network marketing, and even once they have made it, many people have trouble sticking with it. How you approach this situation depends on whether you are the primary wage-earner in your family or not, so I'll approach it both ways as well.

For people who are the primary wage-earner, it's very difficult to put aside that steady check in favor of the less-secure, vacillating check associated with network marketing. It's difficult, though not impossible, to take that leap of faith and step away from the safety net of a corporate job. The good news is that you don't necessarily need to do that. It will slow the rate of your progress but you can grow your business in the background of your full-time job until it grows enough to replace your current income. That process is within your control.

The fact of the matter is that in order to grow your paycheck in the networking profession, you need to invest both money and time. For primary wage-earners, time is often the harder resource to come up with. It's easier to grow your business if you're not concurrently working another job; however, giving up your current job isn't always an option. For that reason, primary wage-earners often have a difficult time growing their business and many of them will give up rather than wait for the dividend over the longer term.

Don't be that person. Don't be the person who gives up too

soon. Remember the doubling penny example. Remember who has control over the high-value activities that bring success. Commit whatever time you can and stick with it. If you can't focus on network marketing in a full-time capacity, then don't. Don't burn yourself out. Master your universe and keep your focus where it belongs. Accept that it will take longer to achieve your goals and that the road will seem to be slower. That's normal. You can have the same success as anyone else; it will just take more time because you don't have the same amount of time to invest up front as others.

Remember that this journey is all about your success, not your success as compared to the success of others – beside, you have no control over them anyway. Some people will jump in after you and hit diamond way before you. Our record at dōTERRA is only a few months from start to diamond. But that's not normal. Most people will take much longer. I have people on my team who are nowhere near diamond level, yet they've been with the company almost since the beginning. There's nothing wrong with moving slowly as long as you are progressing in the direction of your dreams.

The problems arise when you see other people enroll after you and then pass you up in terms of rank or income level. I met with a woman recently who has been with the company almost since the beginning, and she's only making around $500 a month while other people who joined at the same time are making very generous paychecks every month. I felt her pain, but I had some questions for her.

"How many people did you share product with last week?"
"None."
"How many events did you host or attend last week?"
"None."
"What about last month? In the last three months?"
"None. None. None."

With answers like that, is it any wonder that the answer to the question of "How much success are you having?" is also "None"? She'd given up her control over her business, or more accurately, she'd gone to sleep at the wheel, and no one else could *make* her have more success.

The point, in her case, wasn't how long she'd been with the company but how much she'd been with the company. She'd signed up early on, but she wasn't doing anything to grow her business, so it wasn't growing. Remember earlier we talked about duplication? One important truth that is illustrated here is that duplication is always at work, 24/7. Your business is either growing or declining; there is no pause button. What you do, duplicates, and also what you do not do duplicates. Her priorities were different, and they didn't involve growing her business. I've met plenty of people like that over the years, and they only have a problem when they decide to compare themselves to others and be discontented by that comparison. In those instances remember that success is not measured by money alone. You have to look at your life holistically. More importantly, you need to recognize that your definition of success is unique to you. It will have overlap with other people, but it's your definition and yours alone. You need to remember your personal "why," rather than trying to focus on the "whys" of others.

Be happy for others when they pass you by, but don't get distracted by them. Don't let their success draw you away from mastering your own universe. There's plenty of success to go around, and you can go out there and acquire as much for which you have the energy and appetite. No one else's success will detract from your own, unless you let it.

Winning Others Over

Those of you who aren't the primary wage-earner, I want to warn you about some resistance you might face from whoever *is* the primary wage-earner. Often a wife is looking at getting into the networking profession while her husband continues to work full-time somewhere. In my experience this is more often the situation for people getting into network marketing. What I typically see is that the husband will be resistant to whatever product the wife is investigating. Husbands often look at the expenses of the business and wonder what this new "hobby" is and why it costs so much. Many husbands look at it as their wife's new addiction, and they resent the product — regardless of what that product might be. They don't understand why their wife is earning money only to have it spent on something that doesn't directly support the family.

This attitude is the byproduct of insufficient education about the business, but don't rush out and try to educate your spouse. You can't control another person's opinions and I've basically never seen that approach end well. Keep in mind that it's difficult to watch a car payment go out the door every month when there's no new car in the driveway to show for it. For those of you in this situation, I offer some hope. Typically, those primary wage-earners change their tune when your check hits a couple hundred bucks a month. Once you start to approach and then exceed self-sufficiency, your partner is likely to pause and relax. At that point, they often get on board and start trying to drive the business, to make it grow. They start to catch the vision of what the business could become, and they add their effort to yours. They also often come around because they or someone close to them has had a powerful, moving experience with the products. In other words, they get educated. We live in a culture of "anti-network marketing" here in the United States, so trying to educate someone through that barrier is difficult. Instead, let the results speak for themselves. When you are bringing in the equivalent of a "car payment" your spouse will take notice in a positive way. Just make sure to bring that primary wage-earner on board before you start to encroach on the primary salary. Some people can get very testy when your "hobby" starts to generate more income than their full-time job does, especially if they don't love their job.

So stick with it, be patient, and people will come around. Remember, you can't control everything, so just keep your focus and move forward. Resign as the master of the universe and focus on mastering your individual universe.

7. Be the Messenger
"It is always an empty head that swells." —*Coleman Cox*

In the mid-to-late 90s, the networking profession really took off. New companies sprang up right and left, and teams jumped from one company to the next in an effort to find "the next big thing." In order to lure over established teams companies were offering bigger, better bonuses and compensation plans. Keep in mind that most of those companies are no longer in existence so consequently they aren't paying anything to anyone. Unfortunately, due to those compensation plans and the larger-than-life lifestyles that went along with network marketing back then, many of the owners and top producers in these companies began developing "messiah complexes." They began to think and talk like they were the salvation of all mankind. All that talk and attitude is the reason that network marketing has such a bad name. It's taken almost 15 years to crawl back from that stigma, but we're nearly there. I only rarely hear someone complain about the networking structure of the business anymore. We've come a long way.

We're not done yet, however. The nature of network marketing and the success it can bring, still pushes people to inflate their egos. The challenge of staying humble in a profession of so much success is a difficult challenge, but staying humble (and out of your own way) is critical to your long-term success. I call this being the messenger, not the message. When people develop a messiah complex, they stop thinking about the product or the customer and start focusing on themselves instead. They forget the network that got them to where they are and start to think they earned the success all on their own. They begin spending their time talking about themselves instead of teaching about the product and business.

For those who aren't suffering from that condition it seems extreme and obnoxious. The problem is people usually start to suffer a little at a time, and they don't usually recognize it as they slide down into self-aggrandizement. The ego doesn't often balloon up overnight; it grows a little here and there until it can fill an entire conference center all on its own. When you reach that point, it's really hard for anyone to get in close enough to hear you talk about the product.

I can tell you from personal experience that when people come to listen to you speak, they aren't coming to listen to you talk about yourself. When you host a training class, you should be training people about something. That's why people come. Instead of wasting their time by talking about yourself, give the audience what they came for. That's the surest way to get them to come again.

I've heard the saying that **"People are more attracted to the height of your enthusiasm than the depth of your knowledge."** While I believe this statement to be true, you don't need to be a hyperactive whirling dervish, bouncing off the walls, to show that enthusiasm. In fact, being so hyperactive will probably be detrimental to your future success. The point is that people are more likely to catch the vision from your passion than they are from your logic. You can tell them about all the product information and all the business opportunity, but they'll be more moved when you display simple belief and passion, and then get out of the way and let the product do the talking.

When you try to persuade by using your intelligence and knowledge, you are making yourself into the message. By harnessing your enthusiasm to introduce another topic, you allow the real message to speak for itself. You allow your customer to have an experience that will then speak boldly in the future.

Expectations

There are a few major reasons to position yourself as the messenger, not the message. First of all, are you leading with the product? If not, you're wasting everyone's time and violating their expectations. Second, do you really want to be on trial every moment of every day? The message will receive more scrutiny than the messenger. Third, how much of a load do you want to carry? There's so much information out there that you could use up your whole life trying to learn everything.

So, first, we need to talk a little bit more about why you joined the company. Was it for the spectacular compensation plan? If so, I'll say again that you should probably quit while you're ahead and go find a different venture. The networking profession is not about the compensation plan (though money is nice) because you can make money anywhere. Networking is about getting hands on in improving others' lives.

Grocery store employees never get to see how what they sell can change a person's life through proper nutrition and an opportunity to gather the family. Car salespeople never get to see the result of how stepping up to that bigger car let you grow your family. Even doctors don't really get to rub shoulders with their patients and see how a course of treatment is going; they have nurses and physician assistants for that. But as a network marketer, you get to develop close relationships with people and stick with them over the long-term. You get to build a business by making friends and then helping those friends improve their lives, which, of course means that it can't be all about you and the compensation you're getting.

Aside from the compensation plan, what's left in a network marketing company? If you're in a legitimate network marketing company, you have a product or service of some kind to sell. That's the real purpose of the business, the real message. As I mentioned before, when you interject yourself as the message rather than letting the product be the message, you violate the purpose of the business.

I had an experience in my career prior to dōTERRA that really drove this home for me. The company I was working for was having a big, multi-day convention to talk about the product — supposedly. We'd planned the conference well in advance and we'd spent time and money and effort getting everything arranged. We had gone so far as to plan breakout sessions to test the products; then we'd staged product displays and sample stations around the convention center. Everything was set for a great conference.

But it never happened.

We never had a single breakout session. We never sampled a single product. We never even *talked* about the products. Instead, the owner of the company got up and blasted just about everything he didn't agree with, all the while talking about how the product could cure those people. I'm not sure what product can "cure" a religious or political belief, but the owner was very confident about himself and his ability to "fix' the world. Whether he was right or wrong (and I have a strong opinion about that) was irrelevant. The problem was that no one was going to hear what he meant (that the product could cure almost anything) because they couldn't hear past what he was saying (that everyone was wrong if they didn't think exactly the same way he did). Instead of telling everyone about the wonderful products and their proper usage, he had interjected himself as the message. He had twisted the purpose of the convention in order to talk about himself and his ideology. He had made himself the message (and a pariah messiah) instead of allowing the products and trainings to be the message.

The interesting thing to me is that I had believed in the company and its products up to that point. I had been a product evangelist until this man pushed himself and his personal agenda so hard that I was turned away, too. I knew right then that the company wasn't the right one for me anymore — even though the product was great — and I started looking at other options. I can only imagine how people who were less invested felt.

The problem with talking about yourself on the stage is that people didn't come for that. When you host an event, you set an expectation with the attendees. The expectation is that they are going to get something in return for their time. We'll talk about this more in the chapter about benefits, but never forget that people want to be compensated for their time. Hearing about you — unless you are sharing some inspirational experience and have billed the event that way — is not sufficient compensation. Thankfully, the compensation doesn't need to be in monetary form but it does needs to be real. The people who attend your event need to be able to go home after and think to themselves, "This is what I got from that. I'm glad I went"

Compensation for their time can be as simple as offering a new way to share product or promote events. It can be as simple as a physical product sample or some form of informative material, like a brochure or product guide. People want the motivation and inspiration, and they won't begrudge you the opportunity to make them feel warm and fuzzy inside, but they want some substance too. When you host an event, your job is to make sure your attendees get that substance. You need to make sure that you are giving them something that will benefit them directly and in relation to the business and product, not just stories about yourself and your opinions. Save the introspection for when you're mingling after the event.

Your Worst Best Example

Another reason to turn the spotlight away from yourself is that you don't want to be in the spotlight all the time. You might think you do, but you don't. Just look at Hollywood. Any celebrity, pop star, or athlete can tell you that life would be better with some quiet moments of peace. Some love the limelight but most probably do not want the constant scrutiny. Politicians are in largely the same boat. They may love to get up in front of an audience and talk politics but they want to be able to turn that off and be themselves from time to time, too.

The message can't ever be turned off. If you turn off the message, what do your customers and distributors have left? Nothing. If you turn off the message, you ruin them. They will have nothing left to hold onto. Additionally, the message forms the foundation for everything else in the business. Obviously that poses a problem if you decide to turn off the message, and it also poses a problem if you ever need to change the message.

When you construct a culture around a message and then change the message, you shift the foundation from beneath the culture. Perhaps you've seen the demonstration where someone puts a nice tablecloth out, then sets a beautiful place setting. Finally, in a feat of "magic" the person whips the tablecloth off the table, pulling out from underneath everything so quickly that the cups don't even tip over. Imagine company culture like putting duct tape underneath each portion of the place setting, sticking everything to the tablecloth. Are you sure you want to pull the tablecloth out now?

The message, whatever you choose it to be, will form the foundation for everything else your organization does. They will be building on whatever you give them, whether that's you, the company leaders, the product, or some combination. If that foundation somehow changes, you could run into serious problems with the loyalty and motivation of your team. Significant enough shifts in people's perception of the company can turn them away even when they *are* basing their foundation on the product — as with my experience at that convention — so you can imagine how damaging it can be when their foundations are built on something more changeable.

There's another angle to this, which makes it even more important to minimize yourself as the message: your team members will look up to you as an example of what they should be. They'll look to you regardless of how you position yourself in terms of the message; so don't believe that you can escape it. The difference is that when you position yourself as the messenger, you won't be in the spotlight all the time. You'll be able to have down time and time off.

Where I live, for instance, I have trouble even going to the store for groceries without being recognized by dōTERRA distributors. Just the other day I was at a restaurant with Keri and someone recognized us. They had the courtesy not to interrupt our evening, but I got an email the next day pointing out that I'd been seen. Even with all the attention I receive, however, I can still get time off. I can escape the spotlight when I go on vacation or travel to the newer markets. I can redirect the spotlight from myself to the product in order to get a break. Hollywood celebrities don't get that luxury. They are their own message, so they are always in the spotlight.

We naturally assume, though we know it's actually untrue, that our heroes and mentors are the pinnacle of what we hope to be. We see them, and aspire to their level. That's not inherently a problem, but it becomes a problem when those heroes and mentors don't live up to a noteworthy level. The more closely we're tying our behaviors to theirs, the more likely we are to aspire to the lowest (most attainable) level we see them portray. In other words, their low water mark often becomes our high water mark. As a side note, because we are *aspiring* to that level we subconsciously limit ourselves in our attempts to reach that level. We assume that it's out of reach or right at our limit, and reduce throttle when we get close. To some extent, your team members will experience this effect no matter what you do, so you need to always be giving them your best example. However, if you are the message, then you are also their sole source of motivation. If, on the other hand, they have another place to look for the message, they won't be as dependent on you and your example.

By being the messenger, not the message, you can point them in any number of directions to get additional information and examples — often better examples. You can give them a message to build their foundation on without running the risk of leading them astray just because you have an off day (your low water mark) — and you can set things up so that you have days off to have off days in.

No matter what you do, you'll be an example for your team members (good or bad), but that doesn't mean you have to be the only example. By giving them multiple sources for getting information and stepping out of the way, you will help them build a stronger foundation and remain more dedicated.

● ● ●

Death by Encyclopedia

Another reason to be the messenger rather than the message is to avoid needing to know everything. Some people feel like they need to know anything and everything about a business before they can get involved, but that's not the truth. As we talked about before, you can get started with just a little information and grow your knowledge from there.

The same holds true for your team members, although they're likely to have differing needs and interests from you, and you might not have the answers to their questions right when they want to know.

If you are the message, you are setting yourself up as the source for all knowledge. That means that your team members have to turn to you every time they have a question. Your customers have to go to you whenever they need additional information. Initially, being in that kind of a position might seem flattering and powerful to you. You might enjoy having people come to you and value your opinion and information. Eventually, however, you'll come to a point where you get tired of it. Sooner or later, you're going to wish that people were ambitious enough to go and find their own answers. The problem is that you've trained them not to look elsewhere.

Rather than put yourself in that position, be the messenger and carry the message to your customers and team members. Provide them another source (preferably more than one) where they can turn to get additional information. Otherwise you're going to spend all your time studying product material and never have the time to get out there and build your business. Besides just being too much information out there for any one person to absorb and digest in a reasonable period of time, there's no way you can keep up with answering all the questions from a developed, diverse team, especially if your group starts referring their own teams back to you as the "team encyclopedia". Over time, you may build a knowledge base large enough to be able to answer most questions without much thought or research, but you can't expect that right away. Be patient

• • •

and give yourself time to develop. Also, remember that one of your responsibilities as a leader is to coach and develop your team. Teaching them how to find the information themselves is ultimately more valuable to them than giving them the answer to their questions. Rather than inserting yourself as the middleman in every knowledge search, teach your team and customers where to go to find their own answers. Give them tools, rather than just giving them your time.

When it comes to the message, there are any number of things that you can give rather than positioning yourself as more than the messenger. Most companies have plenty of give-away materials to share with others. Interestingly, this can actually boost your credibility. That may seem backwards, but it's true. By giving people something external to yourself, you are giving a second witness. You're giving verification. When you can refer people to an external source to corroborate what you're trying to tell them, people will recognize your personal familiarity with the product and business. Even though you've referred them to something else, rather than answering their question, you will look more like a well-read, educated authority.

Product pamphlets are a great place to start. These are specifically designed to give introductory material and begin to familiarize people with the product. These kinds of materials are usually easily accessible. When people have simple questions, start by referring them to introductory material like this. Once people have gained that initial understanding, shift to material with more information, like books and articles. These materials are usually harder to get into and more time-consuming to read, but they tend to contain more detail and information. Because of the added depth, they take more commitment but pay off in deeper understanding.

Articles, in particular, can be powerful teaching tools. They tend to be written in more academic language but they are often peer-reviewed, which means that someone other than the author took the time to reproduce any experiments and verify the results. Keep in mind that educational materials don't have to be in written form. Audio books and recordings of conferences can also be powerful tools, especially if you know what part of the speech a person needs to fast-forward to. With today's technology, many eBook readers will actually read the book out loud to you. Audio versions of materials are doubly nice for people with a commute because they can turn that commute time into what I call Drive University. I travel extensively, both by car and by plane. On the plane, I tend to try to meet new people and make new connections, but I usually turn the car into a learning opportunity.

Your customers and team members can do the same in order to better prepare themselves to answer their own questions.

The Internet Age

One of my favorite tools is to send people to the Internet. I use this as both a training tool and as a marketing tool. I know what's in my products, but the Internet has been enshrined as the foremost authority on anything and everything. When people wonder what a certain component of my product will do, I send them to their favorite search engine.

When they do the work of looking up the information for themselves, two things happen: First, they learn how to find information on their own. Second, they get an answer they trust. Nobody likes to feel confused or lost, and no one likes to feel uneducated either. We all want to feel intelligent, and one of the most liberating ways to gain that feeling is to learn how to find our own answers. When we can come upon a problem, puzzle it out, do the research, and discover the answer on our own, we feel empowered and intelligent.

By sending people to your outside resources, you are giving them that chance to be empowered. It's not that you don't want them to bring questions to you; it's just that you don't want to have to be on call day and night as a human encyclopedia. You want people to be capable all on their own.

• • •

Additionally, especially in the case of the Internet, we trust things when we find them in "print." When something is put into written words and made available to others, it takes on a life and power of its own. Somebody somewhere believes in it enough to take the time and make the effort to record that information forever. Thanks to this subconscious acknowledgment of that effort, we are more influenced by what we read than we are by what we hear.

Also, especially in the case of the Internet, we tend to believe things when they have a certain critical mass behind them. When someone tells you something you didn't know before, you hear it, process it, and file it away in the back of your brain. When you hear that same concept a second time, you pull out what you already heard and put a gold star on it. Get enough gold stars on there, and you'll believe it no matter how fantastical the idea is. With the Internet, a simple keyword search can return millions of matches — millions of potential sources to cross-reference and support a thought or concept. The more credible those results (sources), the fewer a person will look at before being convinced of the underlying idea.

So, thanks to the credibility of the Internet you can find an answer to all but the most obscure questions within a matter of seconds. Searching online for specific research or studies will build confidence in the product and in their own ability to find answers.

Rather than spending all your time researching and answering questions, you can focus on building your business and offering training. You can help people learn how to find their own answers, thereby empowering them to do and be more than they were before. You also run less risk of making a mistake and turning someone off to your product.

So be the messenger, not the message. Let the product speak for itself and do what you can to support the product in its role.

8. Benefits

"Thousands of candles can be lighted from a single candle, and the life of the candle will not be shortened. Happiness never decreases by being shared." — Buddha

When people find out that I'm in network marketing, they often wonder why. Although much of the stigma against the networking profession has faded, some still remains. When I talk with people, I often run into those vestigial bits of prejudice.

I have two answers for people when they ask me about why I chose this profession. The first answer isn't particularly satisfactory to most people, but it's probably the more important of the two: I'm wired differently.

I've found that almost everyone wants to be their own boss, set their own hours, and take vacations whenever they want. I've never met anyone who would disagree with any of those points. However, most of them know that would mean taking vacation every day, working no hours, and generally getting nothing done. Some of us aren't like that though. We see the challenge of motivating ourselves and working when no one is telling us to and we embrace that challenge. All I can figure is that we're wired differently. We like a different type of thrill than other people, and there's nothing wrong with that.

Not everyone is built with the mentality necessary to *want* to succeed in network marketing, and that's not a bad thing. I love people who don't want to go into the business aspect of the networking profession, and I don't just mean that I love specific people who aren't network marketers. I mean that I love that there are whole classes of people out there who don't want to go into my chosen profession. In the first place, they can still be customers and still contribute to my success and that of my team. And I can still help them meet certain needs.

In the second place, someone must be willing to go and do all those other jobs that I'm not wired for. Network marketing is a different animal, and it takes a different type of person, just like every other career out there. I could never be a doctor or lawyer, for instance, or a mechanic or foreman or politician. I am not only *not* interested in the subject matter enough to pursue a career in those fields, but I'm also *not* interested in the lifestyle of those professions. That said, I'm glad there are other people out there who *are* interested in those things. We need people like that. We need all kinds of different people in the world, and we can all work together to make the world a better place. It's because we're all wired differently that we can all have success in our different professions.

However, that answer for why I love network marketing is unsatisfactory for many people. It's too simple. Thankfully, it's not my only answer. The second answer, the one people want to hear more about, is that network marketing brings a number of benefits to our family and to the members of our team. Just like everyone else out there, I'm driven by a survival instinct and a set of inner needs that I want met. The networking profession just happens to be the best fit that I've found in order to meet my needs and the needs of my family.

WIIFM

We're all, deep down, searching for a profession that matches our innerwiring. Some people sell themselves short and settle for something with a good paycheck but which doesn't match who they are or how they're wired. Other people search their whole lives and never get lucky enough to find the exact right fit. Still others dream about a job involving a huge paycheck and no work. Those people tend to never find that dream job (or become politicians). Most people, however, find a job that largely meets their needs. It may not be the ideal job, but it's pretty close. They can excel at what they're doing and find satisfaction in it. The fact of the matter is that no matter how humble we're all trying to be, we're still all listening to the same radio station in our heads: The WIIFM station, or "What's In It

For Me?" Deep down, at the subconscious level, we're all motivated to seek out whatever is going to improve our lives. We're programmed to seek out things that help us and avoid things that hurt us. We're motivated by what serves our interests. As a networking professional, you can actually harness that inner radio station to help you find your success.

Without being cynical or selfish, we each only have a limited amount of time to do things — 24 hours in a day, 168 hours in a week —and we all want to get the most bang for our buck. In order to do that, you have to choose the activities that you feel most closely align you to your goals. If your current goal is to de-stress yourself, spending an evening in front of the broke box might feel like it closely aligns with your goals. Of course, watching TV all evening never helped anyone get closer to any goal of real merit, but sometimes it feels like it's the only way to unwind and get our minds back.

To take advantage of the WIIFM phenomenon, think about the inner needs of your contacts, customers, and distributors. What do they have going on in their lives, and how can you help them find better alignment between their current lives and their dream lives? When you're trying to get someone to come to an event, for instance, you are competing with the TV, their spouse and children, the work they brought home, the novel they're trying to write, the bathroom they're trying to restore, or whatever else that person has going on in the evening hours. You're asking for an hour (or so) of their time, and no matter how good and humble they are, they will subconsciously compare your offer against all other offers — whatever else they have planned. If you can't answer the question of what they'll get out of going to your even t—how they will benefit personally — they won't go. They need to have a reason or incentive to attend or it's not worth it to them and therefore, less desirable than their alternative activity, no matter what that activity might be.

In terms of what constitutes an incentive, I'm not so narrow-minded as to suggest just giving out money or free products.

Anything can potentially be an incentive, depending on the preferences and interests of the people involved. Some people will be willing to come to your class just to support you. Their incentive is feeling like they've helped you or strengthened a relationship. Others will come because they're hoping you'll mess up or do something funny. Their incentive is laughing and having a good time. It's nice to have people come and support you, but these kinds of people aren't the ones you really want. The individuals you really want are those who really are in it for themselves — people who are looking for how your product can benefit them. That may seem backwards, but you want people like that because they are the people who will actually buy from you. They are the individuals who will use the product. They are the people who will turn around and share with others. They are the people who are listening to that inner radio station (WIIFM) and drawing the same conclusions that you have drawn.

How do you strike that nerve in these people? How do you find out what need you can meet in them? You need to listen. If you just get someone talking and then listen to the person, he or she will tell you anything and everything you need to know. At dōTERRA, meeting that need is as simple as knowing your product information. When the potential customer tells you about a health concern you can let the customer know about whichever oil or blend will help to support the system of the body that is suffering. Whenever possible, you should either give a sample oil to the person or let them try yours. Having that experience right away will only increase the person's interest and the likelihood that you'll have another attendee at your next event.

Just remember that the key is to help the customer see the potential benefit in what you're offering. Initially, your customers know nothing about what you're offering. If they know nothing, they will see no benefits. You want those people to eventually know everything, but you have to take it one step at a time, giving bits of information that the customers want along the way.

• • •

The Eleventh Commandment

I'm fairly certain that the Eleventh Commandment is "Thou shalt not whine." In that regard, it's a good thing it didn't make the cut because as humans, one of our favorite things to do is complain. That's why the advice to just listen to your potential customers is so important. As we've discussed, anyone still breathing has a need that can be met by dōTERRA essential oils. It's just a question of matching the product to the need, showing the customer the potential benefits. If someone is complaining about their allergies, you can talk to them about natural solutions for supporting the body. If you listen to the people you meet, they'll tell you exactly what they want to hear, exactly what they want you to say. In that regard, typically, we complain in one (or more) of three different areas:

1. Health (or lack thereof);
2. Wealth (or lack thereof);
3. Relationships (which are often because of #1 or #2)

In my experience, even total strangers will complain about something within just a few minutes of engaging in a conversation. That means that you can, in most cases, have your bait in just the first few minutes of a conversation. Now, I don't want you to think that I'm trying to give you a sneaky sales tactic when I talk about having the right bait. Keep in mind that what you're really doing is matching a product to a problem. You didn't cause this problem for this person, but you have a solution. In fact, you are doing the opposite of trying to trick or bamboozle a customer. You're looking for a win-win solution. The customer overcomes a problem or challenge and you grow your network and business. That's a benefit to everyone involved. You're not approaching a customer with a product in mind and trying to sell those customers on the solution to an issue that doesn't exist. You're not trying to convince people that they already have a problem. You're helping them find a solution to something they couldn't find a way out of on their own.

Conveniently, dōTERRA offers obvious solutions to the first two categories of complaints, and the third category generally stems from one or both of the first two. In other words, we can often solve — either directly or indirectly — almost any problem a person has. The solution may not always be easy, but it's always simple. For problems with health, we have the products themselves. Essential oils have a long history of being used to treat almost any ailment mankind has ever encountered. We can help with everything from allergies and arthritis to illness and indigestion to weight loss and wakefulness. Essential oils help the body regulate itself and optimize the natural processes built into it, giving a purely natural remedy to almost any ailment. Many people don't know this, and are surprised when they first hear it. Many are doubtful. That's when I rub a little oil on them and let them experience the beneficial effect for themselves. Again, I am the messenger, and the message proves itself.

On the wealth side, the business of dōTERRA can also help anyone who invests in it. If you find someone who is struggling to make ends meet, you can offer the business side as a way to boost income and free up time. Thankfully, the success that comes from dōTERRA's business model is based on selling product, not just enrolling more people and frontloading them.

Relationships usually run really well on their own. Left in a vacuum, most relationships would last forever. They generally start out on good enough terms, after all. It's when life gets in the way and people choose not to invest in their relationships that things start to fall apart. Most often, that time gets diverted to issues with health or issues with work (the mechanism for obtaining wealth). When you help people learn how to better manage their health, you free up their energy to invest in their relationships. The same goes for helping people create an additional or replacement revenue stream. As they grow their business, they'll gain the income they need and the flexibility they want so that they can devote time and effort to their relationships again.

So don't waste your time or that of your customers by trying to tempt them into joining your company until you've identified a need you can fill. You can give all the perfect sales points about why dōTERRA oils, for example, are the best and how they can improve health, but that won't do much for an unemployed person who spends too much free time exercising and eating right. Make sure you ask questions and listen for the answers. As you learn more about people, they will be more inclined to open up to you, and they'll be more likely to share their feelings and concerns with you. You don't have to become best friends, but you have to display a willingness to listen and not judge while they "complain." If you can do that, you'll end up with more customers than you can count. Once you listen to a person—really listen—and demonstrate that listening by being able to explain back what the person told you, you'll gain significant trust in very little time. That, in turn, will give you the credibility to recruit a person to your next event so long as you bait the hook with what they have told you they want to hear.

Features Tell, Benefits Sell

When I started out in network marketing, I learned to do things the wrong way. My whole paradigm was skewed in the wrong direction, and I suffered for it (though I didn't know it at the time). Like so many distributors, I loved my product and what it could do so that's what I talked about.

For those of you taking notes, what a product can do is considered to be a feature of that product. A car, for instance, can go zero to 60 in some number of seconds, has a certain number of cup holders, a certain number of seats, and a certain amount of cargo space. Those things are all features about the car. When you're going camping in your SUV, however, those features can translate into benefits. For instance, being able to do zero to 60 in eight seconds means you can get up to speed and merge safely on the freeway, even while pulling a trailer. It also indicates more power to get through mud and other terrain once you're closer to the campsite. Having 10 cup holders for 7 seats means that you have room for a soda *and* a milkshake, or a soda and a water bottle, for at least three of the people in the vehicle. Having seven seats means you have room for your whole family — or not quite, in my case. The amount of cargo space determines whether you can bring that screened porch to protect you from the mosquitoes or if you'll need to leave that at home.

The features themselves don't really give much usable information for a potential customer until those features are translated into how they benefit that customer. That was my problem when I first started in network marketing. I knew my products, and I could teach about them all day. I also made it a point to know my company's history. I had lots of information to share, but I just wasn't approaching it in the right way.

Instead of trying to wow my customers with all the impressive features I should have first been trying to identify their needs. Features, out of context, are just information. They don't have as much meaning unless the customer is already involved with the company or product. When you lead with features, you are not really educating your customer with any information he or she can use right away.

My approach changed after I attended a seminar with Randy Gage, who taught me about the difference between features and benefits. He taught that features don't matter to a new customer until that person has a reason to care. Or, as the saying goes, **"Features tell, benefits sell."** (You could also rephrase this as, "Facts tell, stories sell.")

Features are great. I don't want to imply that you shouldn't share the features of your products. However, I also want you to realize that the true power of any given feature is in how that feature improves the life of the customer. You need to identify how your features solve problems for your customers. That solution relationship between a feature and a problem is called a benefit.

• • •

Let me give you an example. Oregano oil has amazing abilities. In World War I they actually used oregano oil when certain medicines were not available. In fact, in studies oregano has been shown to be very effective in supporting the body's natural immune response and because it's a natural substance, it's easier on the body.

Okay. That's good information, right? I outlined some nice features of one of my products. Do you want to run out and buy it now? It you don't, it's probably because you don't have an infection that requires an anti-biotic right now and you're having trouble connecting that product and its features back to your own life.

What if I pointed out that in a natural disaster, one of the biggest killers is the aftermath and the lack of proper medical attention. Injuries get infected and people who survive the initial disaster end up dying anyway because they often can't get treated. Even simple household accidents like cuts and scrapes can end in crippling infections. By keeping essential oils in your medicine cabinet you can be prepared and have greater peace of mind. You can know that you have a powerful substance to support the body's natural defenses.

How's that? A little more convincing? The key is to connect the feature of your product back to a need of the customer. When you make that connection, you'll be showing the customer how they can benefit from the feature.

A Benefit and a Responsibility

A truly wonderful benefit of the networking profession in the quest for wealth and financial freedom is that you can build your own business and make your own success. You don't have to rely on anyone else, and no one else gets to decide how big or small your paycheck is going to be. That happens to be the biggest challenge as well, but it stands primarily as a benefit. It's a challenge because it means that your paycheck is tied to your efforts. If you don't work, you won't get paid. There are no "seat miles" in this profession. You don't get paid just for showing up every day (though showing up every day is a critical first step). Some people aren't willing to make that kind of commitment, and they tend to wash out before they find the real success.

As I've said before, if you just want money, find a job somewhere else because that won't be enough motivation to succeed in network marketing. You've got to be committed to building a business based on a network of people and that takes a huge investment of time and effort before it starts to return any real money. To be successful in this profession you need to be committed to something more than money. For many of our members at dōTERRA that commitment is family. It might be to raise their family out of a cycle of poverty they've been stuck in for generations, or to gain the flexibility to spend more time at home with the family. Or it could be some other reason altogether. Others are committed to some external cause. We have several charitable ventures that we're involved with and dōTERRA actually established a whole charity arm of the business called Healing Hands to promote wellness and to assist the disadvantaged.

Another reason you need a cause like this is because money isn't an end unto itself, not really. If you had all the money in the world, what would you do? If you build your network and stick it out through the tough times just to get money and then you get money, what are you going to do next? What will you do after your network is producing more than enough for you to survive? Will you start buying big toys or blow the money on gadgets and garbage? Eventually, you'll have all the material possessions. What then? Will you waste your money on lavish parties and live life like a rock star? That's just a recipe for burning out and ending your life empty inside.

Money has no intrinsic value. Money only has worth because it serves as a means to attain other goals. Money is something of a measuring stick, nothing more and nothing less. So you need to have a reason for getting into networking that runs deeper. Why do you want the money? What are you going to do with it? If your root desires are purely selfish (fast cars and big houses), you are unlikely to have the staying power when things get tight. If your root cause is deeper and tied into principles and values, you're much more likely to make it to that level of success. You're also much more likely to continue to enjoy life once you get there.

I've stood in front of conventions and told tens of thousands of people that no one needs to make $100,000 a month. I get a lot of laughs at that because everyone *wants* to make that kind of money, but I'll say it again, "No one *needs* to make $100,000 a month." Far too many people survive on less than $100,000 a *year* for me to ever accept that anyone needs more than that per month. Yet some of us make that and more. What good does it do to make so much more than you need in order to survive — more, even, than you need in order to thrive?
The benefit of that kind of money is that it gives you the leverage to go out and do those things you really want to do. Money becomes a form of power, or a tool, which you can use toward accomplishing whatever purpose you choose. Having that kind of money enables you to fulfill your "why" but it also comes with some strings attached. There is a quote which was popularized by one of the Spiderman movies but which has its roots in Voltaire, and even the New Testament of the Bible. It says, "With great power comes great responsibility." The benefit of making so much money isn't just so that you can buy 14 cars and six houses. That would be an abuse of such a blessing. Every person who walks the face of this planet has the chance to change it for the better, and we all share the responsibility to make those positive changes whenever and wherever possible. Making so much money helps to magnify that ability and responsibility.

To be fair, I have somewhat turned this responsibility over to my wife. My time is pulled in many directions, so she has taken over the charitable arm of our business. Often she's written checks for worthy causes — without even talking to me. She'll see a story in the news about someone needing an expensive surgery and being unable to pay and she will write a check to help pay for the surgery. Thanks to her efforts we've donated to many different causes and organizations. She is more attuned to the needs of others and I know she makes good decisions.

I don't share this information to try to make you think we're so wonderful. In fact, I'm trying to do just the opposite. I'm trying to emphasize the true root of the quote, "with great power comes great responsibility." It comes from the Book of Luke: "For unto whomsoever much is given, of him shall be much required…" (12:48).

One of the benefits of success in network marketing is money. Once you've been blessed with success, it becomes your moral responsibility to be a blessing to others.

Financial Freedom

One of the things that I often get asked about is "financial freedom." Some people want to know how far they have to go to get financial freedom; other people want to know what financial freedom really is and what it looks like. The second question is somewhat personal and relative. What counts as financial freedom to one person doesn't necessarily count as financial freedom to another. You may think financial freedom entails being able to pay all your bills on time each month. Someone else might consider it having their house and cars paid off, money in the bank for the kids' weddings and college, and some investment holdings for a rainy day. What financial freedom is to you is really a question of what you need in order to sleep well at night. You are financially free once you stop worrying about money, and most people can manage that on far less than they think.

The catch is that the answer to the first question (how far you have to go to obtain financial freedom) is tied directly to the answer to the second question. How far you need to go is a question of your destination. Thankfully, regardless of your end goal, the process is the same, the inputs are the same, and the outcomes will be the same. In any case, something that might help you understand financial freedom and how you can obtain it is a graph I learned about some years ago. The graph represents the population of any given place and stretches the people out by income in a least-to-most manner. It shows the standard continuum from poverty on up:

This little graph is pretty self-explanatory, but indulge me for a moment. You have "poverty" clear out on the left and "getting by" in the middle. Most of us sit on the continuum somewhere between those two points, though some of us are just a bit to the right-hand side of the "getting by" point. Conveniently, no matter where a given individual falls, the continuum looks basically the same from place to place.

Now, looking at that graph where would you put "wealth?" How far along the continuum would you have to be away from "poverty" before you'd feel comfortable saying that you have "wealth?" If you're like most people, you'd place wealth out at the far right:

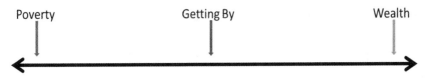

This helps to explain why so few people ever get to the "wealth" point. It's so far beyond where most of us start that it's hard to comprehend getting that far. It's so far away that we have to wonder if it's even worth reaching for, so many don't even try. Besides, it's not like we're suffering now. Not really. We're "getting by," right? We're making ends meet, and that's good enough. It's sort of comfortable here. We're not starving or going without clothing. There's nothing overly uncomfortable about our current situation, so why should we take the risk of stretching clear out there for that "wealth" point?

Now can I tell you a secret? The truth is that wealth is not clear out at the right-hand side. Not even close. The graph is wrong. The actual point of wealth on the graph might surprise you:

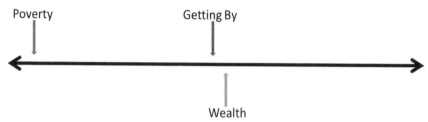

Wealth isn't way out on the spectrum the way people so often think it is. Wealth is just a question of making a little bit more than you need. It represents doing just that little bit more than the *status quo*. It means doing those day-to-day activities that duplicate your efforts. It represents a commitment to not settle for a life of mediocrity like the masses have. Some people need more, and some people need less, but everyone has some income level that would meet all their current needs. That is your "getting by" point. But if you want to be wealthy and have financial freedom then you just have to make a bit more than you need in order to get by and (here's the critical part) SAVE IT!.

Most people, when they do get a raise and start to make a little more tend to increase their expenses to match their incomes. All that does is keep you at the "getting by" point. If you get a raise and immediately increase your consumption to match, you aren't leaving any money left over any more than you were before the raise. You might have more fun, new stuff, but you aren't any freer than you were before the raise.

This is the most common misconception about financial freedom and wealth. It's not about the amount of money you make. You'll never be able to make more than you can spend. That's one of those unwritten laws. Look at the pro athletes and movie stars. How many of them make millions and more per year yet end up bankrupt within just a couple years of retirement? If you allow it, your lifestyle will easily keep pace with (or outpace) your income. The only way to obtain true financial freedom is to discipline yourself to keep your lifestyle in check. If you can raise your income without gobbling it up on lifestyle changes, you'll gain true wealth.

So, again, the key isn't to suddenly find yourself making hundreds of thousands of dollars every year. All you need to do is make a little more than you need to survive. How much do you need to survive? That's a personal question, one you should discuss with the significant other(s) in your life. Get on the same page about what you need in order to survive, and put that number in writing. You can do this through any number of different budgeting techniques; you'll just need to find one that works for you. Once you know your target, keep it there. Don't let it slip upward as you start to make more money. Be disciplined, and the moment you are making more than that number, you'll be experiencing the initial stages of financial freedom and wealth. If you stay disciplined, your wealth and freedom will only grow over time at an accelerating rate.

That's the real secret to getting rich and it's the reason that "get rich quick" is a fantasy. Don't worry about the hare in the race of life. Be the tortoise and keep moving forward one Vital Behavior at a time. Enjoy the benefits, use the benefits, teach the benefits, and then relax and let them work for you.

9. Distraction

"Things which matter most must never be at the mercy of things which matter least." —Johann Goethe

I remember an interview with Darren Hardy, the founder of *Success* magazine, in which he said that the average American is distracted once every three minutes, and the number one cause is their smart phone. This is, of course, an average across people, locations, and personalities, so you may be distracted more or less often than every three minutes. Still, the number is as startling as it is alarming.

Why does this matter? Because distractions slow your progress. Can you imagine what it would be like if your car turned off and came to a grinding halt every three minutes? If you live in a big city like New York or Los Angeles, you might not notice much difference. But if you're driving *from* New York *to* Los Angeles, you'd be having a very different experience. Being forced to stop and start again every three minutes would make the journey take probably 10 times as long and that's what distractions do. They divert your attention from what matters and impede your progress. They can also take your eye off the ball and set you up for huge failures that you might otherwise have foreseen and prevented.

Consider our example of driving across the country. You're cruising along at the speed limit, *not* stopping every three minutes, when you notice a huge, gaudy billboard just off the side of the road. You know the kind: flashing lights and too many colors. You look over at it to try to read what it says but you're having trouble because of the font style and the coloring. After just a moment, you give up and look back at the road, but you're too late. There's bumper-to-bumper traffic just up ahead and you weren't paying attention. You slam on your brakes, but it's too little too late. You rear-end the car in front of you. If not for that billboard you would have been focused on the road, seen the traffic ahead, and slowed down in time to avoid the accident. Maybe you could have changed lanes or taken an exit to stay on track. Unfortunately, that billboard distracted you and the rest is now history.

Sadly, this happens all the time in real life. It usually isn't a billboard. It's usually a text message or an email, a baby crying in the back seat or a friend talking too loudly in the passenger seat. Maybe it's a wreck on the other side of the freeway. In the world of network marketing, any number of things can prove to be distractions. Family and friends can be a distraction, though often that's a distraction we should consider indulging. Success can actually be a distraction when we start to fixate on success rather than focusing on the business. Issues with a company's structure or a problem with a particular product can also be distracting.

In any case, the world is full of distractions and they can prove disastrous if we aren't paying attention and working to focus through the difficulties, so let's talk about some of the common distractions and what you can do to stay focused when life tries to throw a wrench in your works.

Family and Friends

I almost hesitate to list this as a distraction, but it can be, so bear with me while I explain. First of all, I'm *not* trying to say that you should avoid having family or friends because they're going to distract you from your goals. In fact, in general, I feel just the opposite. One of the most effective ways to stay on target is to have family and friends along for the ride. You can all offer support and encouragement to one another. You can share tips and best practices. You can present as product experts for one another.

There are a host of reasons for having family and friends in your life, though not all of them relate to your business in the networking profession. I want to be very clear up front about that though, because I consider my family (particularly my wife) to be one of my best sources of support and focus. My "why" is what motivates me. Much of that "why" has to do with what advantages and opportunities I am able to provide for Keri and the boys. Paying attention to your family and friends can be one of the biggest boosts to your productivity. Having family and friends who support and encourage you will help you keep going through the tough times. They can help motivate you to make one more call or push that little-harder-to-fill-the-room event. That kind of family and friends is great, and I encourage you to have those kinds of people on your side. That said, the unfortunate truth is that not all family and friends are supportive. No matter how much you love them, some people will disagree with what you're doing and they may be very vocal about it.

You'll recall that I had this experience when my parents and in-laws teamed up to give me an intervention. In their eyes, I was wasting time and effort on something that would never amount to anything. In hindsight, they were both right and wrong. That company *did* go out of business, so all that effort didn't amount to much. On the other hand, I am where I am today in large part because of what I learned during my experience with that company. I eventually ended up having enormous success through network marketing. I had insights they didn't have and felt that the networking profession was a legitimate choice for a career. I followed up on my convictions, putting into practice the things we're discussing here, and proved the validity of the industry.

I recount that story because of what might have happened if I'd listened to my family that afternoon. Don't get me wrong, I paid attention to what my parents were saying, and I gave time and thought to the points they were making. However, I had a different view than they did and I stayed true to my view. If I hadn't, if I'd let them change my mind, I wouldn't be where I am today, doing what I love.

I've mentioned before that there's a certain stigma attached to the networking profession. Because of the way some of those companies were structured in the early 90s there's a lot of bad publicity out there surrounding network marketing. That's exactly why I've encouraged you to be careful with which company you affiliate. Don't jump from company to company searching for the "flavor of the month." Find a good company with a good product and good leadership, and stick with it. That's the safest course of action. That way, when the doubters among your relatives come to you and express their concerns, you'll already know whether their fears are valid. When I first started in networking, I had an aunt who was always on my case about whether I'd made any money yet. If you aren't careful, that kind of relative can quickly become a distraction and you'll find your career in a pileup on the freeway because you were looking in the wrong direction.

The way it works is simple: once you start listening to the doubters, your own determination will waver. That's true of any business or endeavor. Try becoming a successful athlete, musician or restaurateur if you allow naysayers to constantly distract you with their "you can't do it" chants. You'll start looking around for all the warning signs and you'll find them. The fact is you'll find whatever negative things you're looking for in network marketing, no matter how great the company and its product are. Once you start to see the "evidence" that the company isn't quite right, you'll tap the brakes. You'll throttle back from all the effort you've been putting in. Once you start to turn down your efforts and pull out, your success will stop. That's not really a surprise since you're not investing anymore; however, in your new state of mind, you'll see the drop off in success as further evidence that the company is false. This becomes a vicious cycle, which will drive you down and take your success with you.

Let me point out something else about his particular distraction. Let's put aside network marketing companies for a moment and talk about "real" companies, "legitimate" businesses. How many small businesses close their doors every year? About half of all startups fail and only a few of the survivors really go on to become anything noteworthy. Most of them just tread water until the owner gets bored and closes up shop.

What about big businesses? How often do they have

problems? Open a newspaper and you'll find a story or two about lead paint or baby formula, workers' union striking over unsafe conditions, a bank failure, another bank exposed for deceptive practices, government constantly losing track of one thing or fouling up something else. I'm not trying to put you in a bad mood, but I want you to realize that every industry and organization is at risk of having negative publicity. Network marketing companies tend to receive more than their fair share but that doesn't change the facts.

So, when your aunt or neighbor or son or best friend from college tells you that you're being crazy and irresponsible, don't let that person distract you from the work you're doing. Don't look aside and start searching out all the dirt they've just warned you about. Instead, continue to make the most of your current opportunity and show the naysayers just how wrong they are.

Family and friends can be a great support, but they can also be a distraction too. So be careful about what you're allowing them to project into your life.

Perks and Prestige

Ironically, another one of the distractions network marketers face comes from the very nature of the job they do. Because they spend so much time focusing on building their business, the success itself can actually distract from additional building activities. People can get so caught up in what they've built that they forget to keep working on it. They forget about maintenance. Perhaps you've seen this in that top producer who goes on to develop something of a messiah complex. Instead of working to help customers and grow team members, the person starts to focus on the paycheck and the triple-diamond, grand-poobah, superman club. People can get so caught up in the glitz and glamour that they forget how they got there and who else had a role in that success. They just want more stuff. They start to think that they can do no wrong. For producers like this, customers and even other team members start to feel less and less like critical members of an effective business organization.

Instead, those critical people start to feel more and more like stepping stones, like a means to an end. Eventually, the network that put the producer into his position can start to feel like a hindrance or a burden — there's too many people calling with too many questions.

Once a person starts to develop this frame of mind, he's more and more likely to cut corners or resort to shady sales tactics to move more product. He might start frontloading, always pushing for that next level, rather than sticking with the simple, effective principles we've discussed so far. A producer in this mode of thought can continue to produce for a while as he exploits what he's built but eventually the person will run out of credibility with the members of his team. Customers will start to feel pushed and taken for granted and they'll start to look elsewhere for the product, or worse, give up on the product entirely. Team members will feel ignored and slighted, and they'll start to talk badly about the negligent producer. All that negativity, in turn, will change the culture and tone of the team, ultimately bringing it down.

For examples of this you need look no further than many of the network marketing companies of the 90s. So many of them were structured in a way that actually encouraged this kind of distraction-by-success behavior. Rather than focusing on the product and the simple behaviors and actions that lead to success, many of these companies focused on the glitz and glamour, becoming self-centered, self-indulgent, bloated and top-heavy, eventually imploding under their own weight. A focus on cars, houses, jewelry, status, trips, and other prizes distracted everyone from the state of the business and the value (or lack thereof) of the product or service. Some of these companies talked up their compensation structure to such an extent that I wonder if it was all just a cover, an excuse to pursue their greed. In that regard, some business owners were very effective at achieving their goals of distraction. Others, however, just fell prey to the environment due to poor planning and controls. Regardless of intent, the fact remains that the owners and the upper echelons of many of those companies ended up being distracted by their own success. They lost sight of the business fundamentals and essential behaviors. They developed the attitude that they could do no wrong, and the companies failed to thrive.

Those failures have helped formulate a story about what network marketing is — a falsehood that has helped skew some public perceptions. Don't let leftover stories of the past distract you from making the most of a great opportunity today. If you really want to have and maintain success in network marketing then you need to discipline yourself starting now. You need to learn to manage your ego and maintain your focus on what matters and why. Again, we come around to see that one of the most important things is that "why" question. Why are you really involved?

If your why is something shallow — like the cars, houses, and trips, or the power and prestige — then you will be much more susceptible to being distracted from the business fundamentals. If your why is rooted in principles of deeper importance, like family and helping others, then you'll have more strength to resist this kind of distraction.

Not *all* focus on perks and prestige is bad, however. Setting a goal to achieve the next level of distribution in your organization can be a good thing. It can be very motivating. Seeing that next tier in the bonus structure and working to get there can be a great way to improve and move forward. The difference is the "why" behind what you're doing. When the focus is solely on the bonuses and rewards, you lose focus on the business fundamentals. When you use the perks to motivate yourself to double down on the fundamentals you can actually use those rewards to help yourself focus and move forward. They can work to remove distractions or at least bring you back from distractions more quickly.

After all, when you see the chance for that dream vacation with loved ones just within reach you're more likely to work hard to get it. When other distractions arise, you'll ignore them because you want to go on that trip. As long as the reward serves to focus you on your business, it's fine. When you start to neglect the business

• • •

fundamentals then the rewards have become too important and you need to course-correct or find yourself crashing.

In the end, it's okay to enjoy the perks and prestige of being successful. You earned it. Just make sure you don't try to take all the credit and glory for yourself and end up pushing everyone else away.

Having Problems

Family and friends can be a serious distraction because they are the people closest to you. They have a direct line to your heart and mind. If a stranger came up to you and told you that you were making a bad choice, you'd probably roll your eyes and ignore the person. It's harder to ignore family and friends. When family begins to criticize and doubt, you have more of a tendency to listen, heightening the chance of being distracted. As we've discussed, even when you fight through it all and succeed, that very success can start to distract you as well.

Both of these distractions – family and success – are dangerous, but neither of them is the distraction you need to stay on the lookout for the most. That's because of all the things that distract in the network marketing profession, the biggest culprit is problems that arise while working your business.

Problems with your business can take all shapes and sizes, but they tend to distract networking professionals the most because they interrupt the flow of business. To an extent, you can ignore family and friends when they try to question what you're doing. You can also ignore the trappings of success and just focus on achieving even more success. Problems, however, force you to stop and look at them. Network marketing is so simple that having something break that straightforward flow is really quite jarring. It's like having a blowout on the freeway. You can ignore the billboards, and you can ignore the gestures of other drivers, but you can't ignore problems that stop your own vehicle.

Some examples of potential problems include having a no-show meeting; issues with the product (out of stock, bad quality, delayed shipment, etc.); or a customer service mistake. If you've experienced anything like this then you know what I mean. If you haven't, just hold on, your time will come. These sorts of issues can easily get right up in your face and be very distracting, if you let them. Occasionally, it will seem nearly impossible not to stop and dwell on them for a while. **The moment you stop, however, your business stops with you.**

If you turn your focus to a hiccup then you're not focusing on building your business through sharing the product and promoting events. Every minute you lose in focusing on a problem is a minute lost forever, so make sure to get yourself back on track as quickly as possible.

That's not the end of the problem, however. In fact, it's not even the worst of it. The worst part is when problems spread. Have you ever noticed how bad things tend to do that? If you smell something good, you stop and keep sniffing at it. Again and again. You'll keep sniffing it until your sense of smell goes numb before you pass it on to someone else. That's how humans are about good things. We look for them so infrequently that when we find something good, we tend to hold onto it. But when you smell something awful, you immediately push away whatever is making the bad odor — generally as far away from your own nose as you can reach and generally right under the nose of someone else. Don't ask me why, but that seems to be human nature. If you smell something bad, you're almost immediately telling your friend to take a whiff.

The same holds true with experiences. If you have a good experience, you tend to treasure it a bit more. People tend to hold onto their good experiences and share them less frequently. Contrast that with a bad experience. When people have a bad experience with a company, they immediately go to social media and blast it out for the whole world to see. Then they go to their family and friends individually and share the experience again, encouraging others to gather around and share in the tale of woe and misfortune.

At that point you've taken your problem and put it in

everyone else's faces. Some people will likely shrug off the problem and keep going with their work. The rest, however, will see your problem and relate it back to a problem of their own. Now, you aren't the only one who is distracted. Congratulations, you've successfully distracted others. Now, everyone is watching the ugly billboard together and no one is watching the road.

The Dog Poop Effect

I call this situation the dog poop effect, and I apologize now for the disturbing mental image that causes. I know it's not the most polite way to look at it but allow me to tell a story and you'll see why it fits so well.

Jim was a guy who loved to go walking in the mornings. He loved the fresh, cool air, and he loved to see his neighbors and say hello to them. Every morning he would get up and walk around his neighborhood. One morning, while he was out walking he noticed something on the lawn of a neighbor who lived fairly close to him. It was a large pile of dog poop. Jim stopped and stared at it. Pretty soon, some of Jim's neighbors started coming around on their own walks. Jim quickly waved them over and pointed out the pile. Within half an hour or so Jim was part of a large-and-growing crowd of the neighborhood all pressing in to get a look at the pile. People started asking questions about the size of a dog that could have left such a mess behind and about the person who would leave the poop on the lawn. And that's when it happened. Someone else showed up at the back of the crowd and tried to push through to see what everyone else was going on about. That push sent a ripple through the group and into Jim's back, knocking him forward. Off balance, Jim put a foot out to stop himself from falling and stepped right in that pile of dog poop. Yuck. Pretty quickly, everyone cleared out, but Jim was still left with dog poop all over his shoe.

Now, how could Jim have avoided the situation? First of all he could have cleaned up the poop when he first found it. Then again, it wasn't his dog, his lawn, or his responsibility and he might not have had the resources he needed to clean it up. But under no circumstance did he have reason to call anyone (let alone everyone) else over to gawk at it. He could have just walked right by and not made a big deal about it. If he'd stayed focused on his walk and on greeting his neighbors instead of letting himself get distracted by the dog poop and distracting everyone in his orbit, he wouldn't have been there to get pushed into the middle of something that wasn't really his concern.

On the other hand, this story is a perfect example of how a minor problem can quickly snowball into a major problem if we keep focusing on it. We all know what dog poop looks like. We know what it smells like. There is nothing exciting, new, or edifying about dog poop. Dog poop will never build you up in any way. You can't even use it as fertilizer like cow manure. It's the same with problems in business. We all experience them. We've all had a shipment come late — or never come at all. We've all experienced poor service or had an employee somewhere at some point tell us something wrong. We've all received the wrong product with no time left to exchange it.

Bad things happen. There's no dispute about that. The key is to not let problems derail you. The path to success is simple. Just keep talking to people about the product and keep promoting events. Problems are nothing more than speed bumps along the way. There's no reason to let a speed bump turn you into a wreck. Even more importantly, there's no reason to let a problem compound and take control over your entire life — or the lives of your friends, family, customers or team members. Everyone else is looking to you as an example. Don't be an example like Jim. Don't call everyone over to talk about a problem. Instead, be an example of the person who perseveres in spite of obstacles. Show your true colors by pushing through problems. When issues do arise (because they will), do what you can to fix them and then move on. Don't dwell on them or draw attention to them. Additionally, when you see other people congregating around a fresh "distraction" pile, do what you can to remind them of the task at hand. Don't join them and commiserate about how the shipping department messed up an order. Instead, go and redirect the conversation. Help them remember what their purpose is. Help focus them. Help turn their attention back where it belongs: on using the product, teaching about the product and repeating that process. Help them focus on the vital behaviors of sharing and promoting. Neither you nor anyone else is going to get anything out of sitting around the water cooler and complaining. In network marketing, you're paid for your results, not your time.

If you want to get paid, you need to go out and get results. That means you don't have time to sit around and philosophize about things outside your control. When the networking companies I was associated with in the beginning developed problems, we didn't sit around and talk about all the things we'd seen which must have led up to their failures. Instead, we found a new home and went to work.

Distractions just waste your time. They're enticing in the moment, like foul gossip, but they'll leave you penniless and bitter at the end of the day. Shrug off the negativity and focus on what matters. Push ahead and leave the dog poop behind. Don't turn over control of your success to a problem outside your control — and if the problem is inside your control, then fix it and move on.

10. Leadership

"The task of leadership is not to put greatness into humanity, but to elicit it, for the greatness is there already." —John Buchan

Leadership is critically important in the networking profession. Effective leadership will catapult a company into the forefront of its field while ineffective leadership will result in lost time, lost effort, lost profits, and lost hope. Leadership is so critical that it can make or break a company, and it takes a number of different forms.

The most obvious form of leadership is you as a leader of your own team. As mentioned previously, in a traditional corporate job you join as part of the base of the organization and have to work your way up. The only way to move up is if someone above you dies, quits, or gets fired. None of these is a particularly happy situation. In limited cases, the company can grow enough to open up new leadership positions, but this is infrequent. In the networking profession, however, you begin at the top of your own organization. You don't have to wait for someone to die or quit in order to move up, you just build your own organization. As the head of your own team you need to be an effective leader to help your team grow and thrive.

Another obvious form of leadership is that of your upline support team, and in parallel, the leadership capability of your own organization. In traditional business you look up the chain of command for help and answers when you have problems beyond your experience. In the networking profession, you have the advantage of being able to look in both directions for the wisest advice available. Your leaders have been in the company longer and likely have more experience than you, but your own organization's leaders are also leaders of their own teams. They are wrestling with the same challenges that you are, and they have plenty to teach you, if you'll let them.

• • •

A less common way of looking at leadership has less to do with how you manage others and more to do with how you manage yourself. Maybe you've had a boss or coworker who violated this principle. The person is a brilliant director, energizer, strategizer, and motivator, but can't keep his own life in order to save it. That kind of person always comes across as a bit "off" and it's hard to want to follow someone when his actions speak so much more loudly than his words.

The final aspect of leadership is just as obvious as any of the others, yet it tends to be one we overlook. When we think of executives, we automatically think of them as leaders. After all, they are in charge of the entire company, right? One of the things we don't always consider, however, is how that leadership will affect us, both directly and indirectly. What kind of organization is the leadership building? What kind of development opportunities do they provide? How do their personalities fit with one another (if there is more than one executive leader), how to they blend to function for the whole company, and how do their personalities mesh with your own? Are they people with whom you would choose to spend your spare time?

In network marketing, the executive team we "hire" to be above us (by joining their organization) can created a lot of the happiness or misery we experience in our day-to-day affairs. That being said, we are responsible (not our leaders) for our success. There are many examples of successful builders who had little support from "leaders." If you don't have the leader you wish you had then become that person, become that leader.

As you focus on leadership in its many facets you'll be better equipped to handle the challenges that life and the workplace can throw at you. You'll be a more complete person and you'll have far more success.

Let's take a deeper look at the three different aspects of leadership and how they apply to you.

Being a Leader Yourself

The first aspect of leadership for you in network marketing is your position as a leader of a team. That team is comprised of you and those that you have brought into your organization and who report through you into a larger team, run by your upline leadership. The effectiveness of your team is largely determined by you. Specifically, there are two major areas that you will affect as a leader: team culture and individual development.

No one should underestimate the importance of team culture. As the team leader, it's up to you to set the tone and positively contribute to that culture. If you don't take an active hand in building that culture, you'll end up building it by default and a default culture isn't normally as positive as you would like. Do you want a team that's driven by profit and dollars, where the ends justify the means? Do you want a culture that tolerates laziness, lying, backbiting, or internal competition and its attendant strife? Or do you want a team where people look to help each other, even at personal expense, to grow the whole team together? Your choice will affect the way you approach your position as a leader. It will also influence the kinds of people you recruit and how you focus your training. Personally, I think that focusing only on profits is a shallow way to look at your culture. If you want a position that's all about numbers and profit, go get a job with a Fortune 500 company. In my view the whole purpose of the networking profession is to enable you to bring the family back into the work sphere — or bring the work sphere back into the family, either way.

If you think about it, 200 (or even just 100) years ago, we lived in an agrarian society. People interacted with one another and helped each other, but the real core of the business enterprise was the family working together out on a farm somewhere. I'm not advocating that we all abandon the cities and suburbs, move to the middle of nowhere, and begin subsistence farming. I think we've made a lot of progress since those days. At the same time there is a lot of value to having your family in your business with you, both to your family and to you.

Your family benefits by having you with them more often. Your spouse will benefit by seeing you more often and being able to learn and grow alongside you. That should help to mitigate the communication problems that seem to plague our society today — when couples suddenly find that they have nothing in common. If you're working side by side, you'll always have things in common.

Your children also benefit from the business by learning important skills earlier in life. They'll learn the values of discipline, diligence, and integrity. Additionally, they'll get to see what it's like to work as a self-employed entrepreneur. Rather than watching their parent(s) drive off in the morning and come back at night (which doesn't really look very difficult), your children will see the time and effort you put in, and they'll better appreciate the whole enterprise as a result.

Your extended family can also benefit by being held together more closely and having that available support network when needed. You can learn and grow together and enrich each other. You will also benefit in terms of having support and encouragement. You won't have to worry about whether your team is playing for the same side as you or not, because you really will sink or swim together. What's more, you'll have something deeper than simple camaraderie or acquaintanceship holding you together; you'll have love, respect, and honesty.

There are so many advantages to having family involved in your team culture, but it's up to you to make that happen. As the leader of your team, you get to make the decisions that will influence the culture. When you host events, will you make provision for children? A "daycare" or some other activity for them? When you are recruiting, will you actively seek out families? Or will you focus on singles who have no strings attached?

The decisions you make will shape your team culture, and the culture of your team members' teams in turn. That's not something that you should leave to chance or default. You need to be making those choices consciously and deliberately and not by default down the path of least resistance.

Your Team Culture

What kind of culture do you want?

First of all, you want a culture where people show up. You want your team members present both physically and mentally. That means that they come to events, and they put away their phones while at the events. Dead weight (people who aren't willing to do anything) is a waste of time and resources, and you don't want that drag on your success. Part of getting people to show up mentally, in addition to physically, is to build your culture on integrity. You want people to do what they say they're going to do, no matter how difficult it turns out to be, whether or not anyone is watching.

Another key element is consistency. You can't cram for business success the way you crammed for a test in high school. We teach people to get two contacts and two follow-ups every day, Monday through Friday. That's not much and shouldn't take that long, but being consistent with it every day will lead to success over time. Like our doubling-penny-a-day example, two contacts every day adds up to over 600 contacts each year. The cumulative effect is fantastic.

By contact, I mean that you are giving out a product sample or tool or some kind of marketing piece about your product or company, in person. That's the easiest way to get the product into the customer's hands to generate a positive experience. Largely, we don't have a way (yet) to transfer product by phone or email, but you can make the contact by phone and follow up by mailing the product sample, if you need to.

By the way, email doesn't count for these contacts. With email, it would be so easy to just buy a distribution list and send out a couple of hundred emails right now. That would meet your two-a-day contact requirement for the rest of the quarter, right? It doesn't really work that way, not if you want to be successful. Email is great for communication with your team or with established customers, but you can't rely on it to build your business. Email is too impersonal, especially when you don't have an existing relationship already in place.

In terms of consistency, I have members of my team who do their 10 weekly contacts and follow-ups in the same day, and then they're done for the week. That works for them, but I still believe that spreading it out a little is more effective. There's a reason I teach 2-a-day contacting instead of 10-a-week.

In the book "Good to Great" by Jim Collins, he tells the story of two competing teams trying to get to the South Pole, one from Norway and one from England. The story is called the 20-mile march. In preparation for this trek to the South Pole, the Norwegians spent months living with Eskimos, training, and gathering supplies. The British prepared by getting some snowmobiles and throwing together a crude plan. But that level of preparation wasn't even the biggest difference.

When the time came to start the journey the Norwegians set a pace of 20 miles every day. No matter what the weather was like, they went 20 miles. If the weather was good, they did their 20 miles quickly and had more time to relax in camp. If the weather was bad, they would move more slowly but still make their quota. The British team set no such pace. Their snowmobiles broke down right at the beginning and they had to go forward on foot. For them, when the weather was good, they would push for as many miles as they could get, sometimes as many as 50 miles in a day. When the weather turned bad, however, they would stop and hunker down — sometimes for days in a row. In the end, both teams reached the South Pole but only the Norwegians made it back. They'd had a few days when the weather was so bad that they had to stop and wait it out, but their 20-mile march of consistency had carried them through. The British died just six miles from a supply outpost on the return journey.

What always amazes me most about this story is the stubborn

consistency of the Norwegian team. Even on beautiful, clear days when they could have easily done more than 20 miles, they didn't. They did their 20 and then camped to rest and conserve energy. They actually made it to the South Pole a full month before the British, even though the British would take advantage of the nice days to put dozens of miles behind them.

This is a perfect example of the Aesop's fable "The Tortoise and the Hare." Success in your team will be achieved through consistency, not through short bursts followed by down time, so make sure your team culture is one of consistency instead of sporadic cramming.

Content Matters

Another responsibility you have as a leader is to provide actionable content to your team members. You need to make an effort to find and teach them things that will enrich their lives. This ties right in with the individual-development concept that I stressed when discussing mastering your own universe. As a leader, you have a responsibility to help your team members develop individually. For example, almost everyone has been to an event of some kind — a work meeting, a professional seminar, a political rally, a church group — where the speaker had a lot of talent for motivation. The speaker was able to talk you up, down, sideways, and upside-down. Everything was so inspirational and empowering and it just made you want to get up, go out, and do something. I love that kind of stuff. Motivational speeches might be my drug of choice — right after frankincense (one of our oils). I love that feeling of being pumped up and hungry. I just wish it lasted longer. No matter how amazing the speaker is, you can only get a couple days of that euphoric energy before it wears off. That "wearing off" is what happened when you got home that night after the speech and thought back, and you couldn't remember what it was that you were going to go out and do. In fact, you couldn't remember much of anything except for how fired up you'd felt. There was nothing actionable to take home and teach to your spouse or children.

If you've had that kind of experience, you know what I'm talking about. If you haven't, just wait. You'll have it eventually. In marketing it's sometimes called "being all sizzle and no steak." In other words, it's all show and no substance. It makes you feel good in the moment but it doesn't leave you with anything satisfying in the long run. A good litmus test for the quality of an event is how many pages of notes you took. Successful people are note-takers. They read, and they take notes. They do that to help their brains categorize and retain information. If you go to an event expecting good information and leave without taking a single note, then the content was missing. If you leave with pages and pages of notes and ideas you know you were well fed.

As a leader of a team, you have a responsibility to make sure that your team is well fed whenever you're in charge of an event. It's true that if you and your team attend a corporate-wide event, you don't control the content. That's determined at the corporate level. However, when you're in charge of the meeting, you have all the control. Choose the content well. One of the reasons that I read so much personal development literature is to make sure that I always have real content to share with my team. I want to fulfill that responsibility to enrich them with actionable information. The goal is to help them become more so that they can do more.

Leading Yourself

The rest of this book is largely dedicated to building your own capacity and capability, but I wanted to take a moment to emphasize that here. You are the leader of your life, and your personal success depends on how well you lead yourself.

So many of us think about leadership as some sort of external force, an almost magical force that people either possess or don't. Hopefully we've already demonstrated that leadership is more than some extra-worldly superpower. I want to make sure you understand that your leadership ability needs to be directed inward. Doing so will help you find and maintain direction. It will also help you develop and amplify your leadership ability toward others.

We've talked again and again about being a self-starter and getting yourself moving. I want to talk about that again for a moment. Why? Because, what motivates you is probably the most important part of the networking profession. For nearly every other job out there, you have a boss who will check up on you and make sure you're doing what you're supposed to. Many jobs will track your performance and fire you for failing to meet targets. In network marketing, you are your own boss. You have to provide that motivation to yourself and you're the only one tracking your performance and threatening to fire you. For some people, the freedom of having no boss is just that: freedom. For others, that freedom is the hardest part of the job.

Life throws so many things at us, and so many of those things seem so important at the time. In a "real" job, your time and effort outside of your job are limited by the nature of your work. With the networking profession, you get to choose how and when you spend your time, but you don't suddenly gain any extra hours in a day. Having that additional freedom to choose can be very difficult because we suddenly feel liberated from long work days and we want to celebrate our emancipation. That's fine. Celebrate it. Then get back to work.

In the normal-job world, any career with upward potential will require 40 hours per week — probably more. Many more. You can maybe get by with less than that in the networking profession, based on how productive you are in those hours, but not by much. If you can't be as focused, dedicated and driven building your own business as you were when you were building someone else's business, then you need to strengthen your "why." You need something more to motivate yourself.

The key is to find a reason that's deeper than simple money. You can make money anywhere, as I've said before, so that's not a good enough reason. Besides, it's hard to make money at network marketing, at least in the beginning. You need to focus on all the other reasons. Maybe you want better health or more interaction with others. The most common reasons generally relate to family and prioritizing to spend more time with family. No man or woman at their time of death expresses regret that they didn't spend enough time at the office.

Whatever your individual reasons for working your business, as you learn to cultivate that "why" inside you, you'll be better positioned to help others do the same. You'll be able to help them discover and cultivate their own "whys." After all, you are probably the most difficult, most unruly person you will ever have to lead. Why? Because you know all the right buttons to push to rile yourself or turn yourself off. You know how to engage your procrastination mechanism and how to put your walls up. No one else knows you better than you.

As you learn to work with yourself and motivate yourself through the daily grind, especially on the hard days, you will be learning the skills and techniques to motivate others. Those skills might not apply in exactly the same way with others as they did with you, but the concepts will be largely the same. We're all different in terms of personality, values, and desires, but we all have the same basic needs.

As you learn to tap into your needs and teach yourself to focus, you'll be learning how to help others to do the same. They'll need to personalize your technique, of course, but you'll be able to coach them through the process and help them avoid some of the mistakes and setbacks you experienced. Most importantly, you'll learn how to make those techniques work on yourself at ever-increasing levels. You'll be able to build yourself up from where you are now to heights you can hardly imagine. You can and will be the best "boss" you've ever had, but it will take focus, discipline, and dedication on your part to make it happen.

Executive Leadership

• • •

When you are looking for a network marketing company you need to look for a good company fit. You need to examine the culture to see if it's a culture in which you will thrive. If you don't fit in, you'll have a harder time finding the resources and support you need and want. No resources and no support mean more pressure on you to make your success all on your own. If you're going to pursue that path, you might as well find a "real" job, because you'll have left the networking aspect of network marketing behind. The whole idea of network marketing is that you help others to be successful and they help you be successful in return. By sharing the load across a large team, you will all have success without the stress.

To determine that culture and fit, you need to examine the executive team. After leaving my first networking company I learned that the hard way. That next startup firm had bad leadership. They didn't know how to run the company and they didn't have the capital to maintain their efforts during the beginning phases. If I'd done my research, I would have kept looking and found something else, somewhere else.

One of the most important things to look at is the ownership structure. How many owners are there, first of all, and how do they interact with each other. Most network marketing companies have one owner, maybe two. The problem with that structure is that it's hard to be the point of the top of the company and not be changed by it. In ownership structures like that, the one or two owners at the top tend to get so much success so quickly that it goes straight to their heads. Think of a thermometer in a cartoon on a hot day. The thermometer starts out normal, but then the heat makes the mercury rise. Soon the thermometer tops out and the very top starts to bulge, then explode. In a matter of seconds the thermometer goes from normal to bursting and broken. Being at the top of the company can do that, too.

We all know the quote: "Power corrupts and absolute power corrupts absolutely" (Lord Acton). As we discussed previously, it's true in business too. So many network marketing companies are run by people who get that power, and it goes to their heads. You can see the same pattern played out in politics. When people start to amass power — even if that power is only imagined — they start to let it go to their heads. They start to abuse that power and think the rules don't apply to them anymore. History is full of examples like this, and many of our greatest heroes are the superhumans who managed to resist the push toward corruption long enough to escape it – people like George Washington, Abraham Lincoln, Gandhi, and Mother Theresa.

At dōTERRA we have seven owners and I love that. My experience has been that if any one of the leaders starts to get a little too ahead of the company, the other six can pull on the reins and bring everything, and everyone, back in line. By having seven leaders we have less likelihood of the company going off track into a place where decisions no longer make sense or are made for selfish reasons. Some companies in our profession struggle with this. They may have, figuratively, installed a revolving door in the executive suite. The chief operators of the company — like the CEO, CFO, marketing director and others — come and go like socks: a new pair every day. The actual owners have messiah complexes and think they can do no wrong. As a result, the owners are constantly rotating the leaders in one door and out the other. Consider the effect that has on an organization.

You want to be in a place where you can count on the leadership to make smart, honest moves to propel the company forward and take you along with it. You want to be able to count on the executive leadership and ownership to be the foundation and bedrock of the company, not the wind and waves smashing against the ship.

If you want to have that kind of leadership in your company then you need to shop around before you join. You won't have much luck joining a company and then lobbying for a change in the holding structure. Company culture is a difficult thing to change so you have to shop for a culture you like and then reinforce that culture whenever you can.

If you ignore this part of the process and align yourself with just any old company then you need to be ready to deal with wide executive swings and tumult at the top. Don't be surprised when the leadership of such a company violates the law and the front doors end up with FTC locks on them. I've seen it happen so I'm much more careful now than when I first started out. It is truly extraordinary to work with a team of executives, as at dōTERRA, that live their business and personal lives in a place of cooperation and integrity.

11. Presentation Skills

"Communication is a skill that you can learn. It's like riding a bicycle or typing. If you're willing to work at it, you can rapidly improve the quality of every part of your life." — Brian Tracy

I'm not sure I could count the number of people I know who are afraid of public speaking but it's a very high number. In fact, I've met people who would probably rather light themselves on fire than stand up in front of 30 people and give a presentation or product demonstration.

I won't argue with the reality of that kind of stage fright, but I will say that it gets easier with time. The more often you present the more comfortable you'll become with presenting in general. The good news is that as you make an effort to share your product and promote your events you'll slowly expand your comfort zone until you can successfully give presentations as well.

It may or may not help you to realize that nothing bad is going to happen to you. No matter how bad your presentation is (or isn't) the worst that can happen is "nothing," even if someone has to get up and leave during your class. If something like that happens, you need to recognize that they might not be leaving because of you. A new baby is born about every seven seconds. Someone dies about every 13 seconds. People get sick all the time. People also have business calls with time zone issues, significant others with less-significant questions, and any number of other potential conflicts. A person could come to your event, fully intending to stay, and then have something come up. That person might even feel so embarrassed about leaving in the middle that he never follows up with you to apologize and tell you the reason.

Of course, some people will leave because they refuse to accept what you're offering. It's actually a good thing when those people leave because they're less likely to waste any more of your time, and you won't be wasting any more of theirs. So don't worry about them walking out either. Ultimately, all you can do is prepare for the most impactful, most effective presentation that you can give, and then sit back and see what happens. You have no control over what other people think, feel, or do, so stop trying to control them.

That said, there are steps you can take to improve your success and increase the likelihood of people attending and staying. We already talked about promoting events and getting people there. In this chapter, I want to focus on things you can do to increase the power and effect of your event once people attend. Specifically, we're going to talk about things you should and shouldn't do, how you can make use of others, and how you should act when you make use of others.

Passionate, But Not Fanatical

First, I mentioned previously that people will be more drawn to you based on your passion for the product than they will for your knowledge of the product. That's very true, but in presentations it's only true to a point. As with everything in life there's a time for moderation.

When you're introducing someone to your product or business, you need to let that passion drip from your words. It needs to flow through you and into that potential customer or distributor. If that person doesn't feel your passion and energy he'll be doubtful about your product, and that means you'll likely lose the opportunity.

One of the hardest challenges you'll face in presenting is throttling back on that enthusiasm. Your audience still needs to see and feel your passion, but you don't want to overwhelm them. Keep in mind that the situation in an event or presentation is different from the situation when you're meeting a prospect for the first time, one on one.

Less Is More

We've all been in the situation where we attended a presentation and the speaker was so passionate that we couldn't really get the message. We've talked about being the messenger, not the message, and we've talked about distractions. These three concepts are all interrelated in terms of staying out of the way so that the audience can learn.

Initially, this may not be that difficult because you probably won't know that much about your product. Once you've been at it for a few months you'll have a greater wealth of knowledge, and you'll want to share it all. That's the burden of knowledge. The more you know, and the more passionate you are about that knowledge, the more you want everyone else to know what you know because you believe it will help them.

How do you one down your belief that your knowledge is critical for everyone? Carefully. It's a hard fight, but it's a fight you need to win. I can host a class nowadays and, if I'm not careful, go for two hours or more. I have to consciously, painfully, reel myself in and maintain a laser focus or my enthusiasm will get the better of me every time.

There are a number of problems with hosting a two-hour event. If you do it in your home that's a long time for people to be there. Your spouse might get frustrated while trying to get the children to bed — especially if you and the guests are laughing together. If the event isn't in your home you have to reserve the venue for that space of time and you're still keeping people out late. Either way, your attendance will drop precipitously when you announce a two-hour class rather than a one-hour class. In fact, it almost doesn't matter how enthusiastic you are or how great your product is. If you announce a two-hour event you can be sure that most first-time prospects are not going to show. That's too big a commitment for something to which they aren't yet committed. You'll still get people to come, but they will be people who are already involved in the business. More importantly, you should

● ● ●

actually *want* to get finish your class quickly. Remember our chapter on the three essential traits of successful products? The best way to sell your product is to let your product sell itself

How can your product sell itself if everyone is still focused on you? So minimize your time in front of the group and get your class over with. Cover the basics of whatever you want to cover — and only the basics — then dismiss the class. Why? Because the real magic is in what happens after the class is over, the learning that takes place after the class. That's when the product can start talking. The initial event is a presentation of basic material meant to engage people and hook their curiosity. After the class, the people who are interested will come to you. So you want to hurry through the event in order to get to the after-party, the event after the class. This is when the interested people will come to you with questions about your topic.

In the event you should only share the basics because you only have time for the basics. When someone comes up to you with a question afterwards, you can share all the rest of the material you wanted to present all along. You can let your enthusiasm off its leash. After your class is over people can get to the product, too. They can check out your display and your samples. They can pick up a brochure or a book or other educational material. If they do have questions, they can ask you.

What you'll find is that most people don't feel comfortable asking a question in a group in the same way that most people don't feel comfortable speaking in front of a group. Instead, they'll save that question and approach you with it afterward.

Unfortunately, that means you might end up answering the same question multiple times. Fortunately, it gives you an opportunity to establish credibility and rapport with that person, increasing the likelihood that she will become a customer or distributor in the future.

Before I really focused on tightening up my classes and getting them out of the way, I regularly strayed into the two-hour zone. Now that I'm making an effort to get out of the way, I usually conclude in about 45 minutes. That means more time for questions. It also means that people can leave if they have other commitments and they don't have to get up and walk out in the middle of my presentation if the need arises. It also means that more people come because I invite them to a 45-minute event. That sounds so much better than two hours, doesn't it?

In the past, my 7:00 p.m. classes would run until 9:00 p.m. or so, and people would hurry out after we ended because they had other places to go and other things to do. Now, we finish up before 8:00 p.m., but we still have people hanging out until well after 9:00pm. The difference is that now they're hanging out because they *want* to, not because they have to. And, those who remain late are the individuals who are indeed interested, exactly the people with whom I want to speak. I love it. I have plenty of time to help them discover different product samples, answer questions, and get them enrolled.

By learning to stop yourself from clogging the night with verbal effluent (you know what I mean), you'll be able to take less of people's time. In return, they'll give you that much more time because they feel respected and valued. More time means more chances to find a need and offer a solution.

The Five Senses

During your presentation, if possible, and afterward for certain, you should be involving as many of the five senses as you can — as many as your product allows. At dōTERRA, that's basically all of the senses. People can smell, see, hear about, taste, and feel the essential oils. Not all products will work to touch all five senses, but you still want to rally as many as you can.

Think of each sense as a different channel into the brain (because they are). When you're trying to get people interested in your product you want to reach out to them in as many ways as possible. We've all heard the concept that everyone learns best according to a different sense; you want to connect with people no matter which sense they prefer. The unfortunate reality is that most of us default to using the sense of hearing to transmit a message. We sometimes augment with vision. Think about the last presentation you attended. The speaker talked to you (making use of your sense of hearing) and probably showed some slides or props (rallying your visual centers). We're all used to that. We experience it all the time.

We get bombarded by so much aural and visual interference during the day that we've collectively developed some pretty powerful filters to screen things out. If you only use the auditory and visual senses for your presentation, you're at risk of being screened out as well.

But when was the last time you put something in your mouth and "screened out" how it tasted? When was the last time you held something new in your hand and ignored what it felt like? When was the last time you caught a whiff of something outside that local diner and turned off your sense of smell?

Sometimes we wish we could tune out these senses (like when you drive by a dead skunk on the highway or have to eat something nasty), but the fact is that we don't have those same, sophisticated filters in place because those senses don't receive the same, constant assault. These senses don't need the same defenses. If you can get people using these other senses, they'll have a much deeper experience because they won't be able to filter what's happening during your presentation. There will be less sensory competition in their brains, and they'll be able to process and retain more of the information related to the experience — especially if you can engage the sense of smell.

The sense of smell is one of the most sophisticated senses in the human body. Smell actually accounts for most of your sense of taste. At best taste can only identify sweet, salty, and bitter. The actual tastes of the foods you eat are more a factor of your sense of smell than your sense of taste. If you don't believe it, plug your nose and have someone give you food samples blindfolded. You'll be shocked that you can't tell what you've been given. Smell really is your go-to sense.

We pass oils around for people to smell during the presentation, and afterward we give them the full sensory experience. The ability to rally these additional senses is just one more reason to make sure that you are getting through your presentation quickly. The sooner you finish your class, the sooner you can get to the hands-on component where people get to try out the products.

As I mentioned previously when we discussed the three essential product traits, the best thing you can do to get a new customer is to get your worthwhile product into the hands of that customer. The best time to do this is before the event. Whenever possible, you want to give your customers an experience with the product before they attend. If they've already had an experience, they're more likely to attend and they're more likely to pay attention once they're there. After all, in today's world, getting people to the event is only half the battle. Texting, Twitter, Facebook, and the latest gaming app will all be vying for the attention of your audience.

When they've already had that product experience, they will come looking for explanations and understanding. They'll want to know why the product affected them the way it did. They'll want to know how they can have a similar experience again in the future.

What counts as a product experience? You need to identify a need that the person has and then meet that need. For instance, we have a product that works to soothe headaches. With the pace of society today, almost everyone gets headaches. When a potential customer tries a little bit of this blend, which is all that's needed to help a headache subside, they have just had a product experience.

To put into perspective just how powerful this can be, let me tell you a brief, true story about a gentleman in Las Vegas who was introduced to one of our essential oil blends. This blend is a combination designed to relax muscle tension and stress. People often use it after working out to reduce soreness or to counteract occasional joint and muscle discomfort. This particular man had a

* * *

shoulder issue that periodically left it frozen and nearly immobile. When he used the oil on his shoulder, the joint opened up and began moving again. He was so moved (literally) by the experience that he drove six hours to our headquarters in Orem, Utah to buy more of the product.

Depending on your product, customer experiences can be that strong, or stronger. When you really hit a home run in matching a customer need to a product benefit, you will give that customer an experience that she never forgets. If the man with the locked shoulder had been offered a different product, he wouldn't have driven those six hours to buy more. He'd have gone on with his life without another thought.

When you can harness your customers' senses to give them a multi-faceted product experience, they will be much more likely to attend your presentation and focus on what you're saying. They'll also be more likely to share their positive experience with others and bring them along for the event.

Use an Expert

In your events, especially when you're first starting out, you will often have someone else give the presentation for you. Primarily, you won't know the products or the business that well yet, but there's another reason to use an expert.

In the first place, when you're starting out, everyone will know you're just starting out, and that's okay. You want people to know that you have found something new and that you're excited about it. That passion will be a great advantage for you. At the same time, because everyone knows you are just starting out, they also know that you don't really know about the business or the products. Your knowledge will be suspect by default, making it difficult to get people to act on the information and experience you have — especially people who already know you.

When you start in a new venture, your family and friends will have the belief that you don't really know what you're talking about. They'll most likely be right at first, but, as you grow and develop, you'll outgrow that perception. Unfortunately, they won't.

In the New Testament of the Bible, Jesus remarks that, "A prophet is not without honor, but in his own country, and among his own kin, and in his own house" (Mark 6:4, KJV). In other words, no matter how amazing you might end up, your family and friends will always be your family and friends and they'll always remember all the things you fumbled in past years.

This doesn't mean your family won't love you, support you, and possibly join you; it just means that initially they are going to naturally, subconsciously be skeptical of anything you try to tell them. They will doubt your instructions even though they don't doubt you, and they'll do it without even thinking about it. I knew a young man who was top in his university class and went on to be top in his law school class. He got one of the highest bar exam scores and began practicing law with a big firm. Four years into his practice he overheard a legal problem at a family dinner and because he had developed an expertise in the field, piped up and offered his legal advice. His aunt smiled and thanked him then went out the next day and hired a "real attorney" to get his advice.

I had this same experience with a member of my family. I was asked about how to treat a certain ailment, and I gave a very specific, clear, correct answer. Of course, the family member did nothing. What really makes me sigh about this story is something that takes us into the second half of the reason for using someone else in your events. For whatever reason, people are more likely to listen to a person they don't know than they are to listen to a person they do know — so long as the stranger is credible.

Consider, for example, the last time a loved one told you something and you went to the Internet to verify it. You love that person but you couldn't believe what he or she said without going to a source you don't know (on the Internet; ironically the credibility of the Internet is dubious at best) and getting verification. With my family member, I had a follow-up experience where Dr. Hill, our corporate expert and lead researcher, was in town. I was able to get Dr. Hill and this family member together, and the family member posed the same question to Dr. Hill. Of course he gave the exact same answer I had given — almost word for word. I felt vindicated. Then my family member responded positively and actually followed his suggestion, which then made me feel an inch tall. I had said the exact same thing already, but my family member hadn't even tried out my advice.

My problem — and the problem of every person out there — is that there are two characteristics in play in any persuasion situation, and I only had one of them. In order to successfully touch someone and persuade them, you need an environment of both trust and respect. You need to believe that a person will be honest with you, and you need to value what that person says.

Unfortunately, with family, you will usually have trust without respect. They love you and know that you wouldn't lie to them or try to fool them purposefully (hopefully), but often they still may not take you at face value and act on what you say. To them, you're the one who spilled the punch bowl on mom's new, white carpet; backed the car over the mailbox; or put dish soap in the dishwasher and turned the kitchen into a bubble bath.

Whatever mistakes you made while growing up, your family and friends will know about those things and that will make them suspect of your advice. They will still trust your good intentions but they'll second-guess your expertise.

With an outside expert, you're likely to have respect but little trust. You may believe that the person's advice is sound — so long as it's not misdirected. You'll believe that the person knows what he or she is talking about, but be hesitant to accept that it necessarily applies to you and your specific situation.

The key, then, is to combine people's trust for you with their respect for outside experts. That's how things really worked with Dr.

● ● ●

Hill and my family member. If the two of them had met at random, my family member wouldn't have been as quick to accept Dr. Hill's words. However, I made that introduction, and my family member's trust and goodwill for me now included Dr. Hill through my recommendation. That enabled Dr. Hill to wield both trust and respect and make a profound impact in my family member's life.

That's how using an expert works. You have a vast array of people you know, people who trust you. When you bring in an expert and make that introduction, you lend your trust to the expert and allow your friends and family to be touched by both trust and respect.

Interestingly, the "expert" doesn't actually have to be a true expert in the traditional sense. Sure, any credentials help establish credibility, but you can call in anyone to be an expert as long as your audience doesn't know the person. You can call in someone from your upline, downline, sideline, or even from corporate. Just about anyone can be an expert on something; you just need to set them up that way.

And people aren't the only experts out there. As I mentioned in the section on being the messenger, rather than the message, you can use any number of other tools as your expert. You can share a product guide or informational text, an audio CD, a DVD, or some other form of media, and it can serve as an expert. If you try to tell people about a product application and they don't listen, then you can give them some type of informational material, which shares the same advice. Surprisingly, people will be much more likely to follow the instructions of that "expert" even though it isn't even a person.

The proper use of this concept of trust and respect is of critical importance, especially for newer team members. It can save you much heartache and wasted time. Use it and master it.

Edification

When you invite an expert to come and speak to your class you need to do something critical to help establish that person as an authority and transfer the trust the audience feels toward you to the presenter: you need to edify your presenter. This serves multiple purposes; it helps to boost the confidence of the presenter (who may or may not be comfortable in front of an audience) and gives you the opportunity to establish the speaker as an actual expert in some way.

In order to be effective at this, you should probably talk to your presenter beforehand and find out some information about that person. You don't need to give a 20-minute oration about the person's divine qualities — in fact, you shouldn't spend more than a handful of minutes at the most. All you need to do is give a brief introduction that focuses on a couple of traits to add credibility. All you're really trying to do is boost your expert's credibility. Your audience members know, respect, and trust you on some level, or they wouldn't have come. They don't know, respect, or trust your presenter, however, so you need to transfer their respect for you onto your expert. You do this by edifying the speaker, by vouching for the speaker.

You do this by talking about anything relevant. You can mention educational background (especially if the speaker has an advanced or related degree), work experience (tenure with the company), or work success ("achieved diamond status). Your sole purpose in this is to bolster your speaker and then get out of the way.

Edification doesn't end there. Edification is a two-way street. Once you've stood to introduce and edify your speaker, the speaker should turn around and thank you graciously, taking the time to edify you in return. This reciprocity also serves multiple purposes. In the first place, it demonstrates good will and character on the part of the speaker when he or she is able to graciously accept your praise. Additionally, the reciprocity reinforces you as a good person. In all likelihood, at least several of the people you invite to any given event will hardly know you. You've made an initial connection with them (that's why they came), but your relationship is still probably very new and weak. When the expert gets up and praises you, your guests' opinion of you will rise too — as long as the praise isn't excessive or contrived.

This is also a great opportunity to reinforce you with people who *are* close to you. For example, if you went around praising yourself, people would think you were self-serving and egotistical, especially your family and close friends. When someone else praises you, however, those close relationships can't dismiss the information so easily.

What's more, reciprocal edification will serve to boost your personal confidence. It's almost always more impactful to hear something positive about yourself from someone else than it is to hear that same thing from yourself.

My caution to you here is to be careful that you don't drink too much of that Kool-Aid. People — especially close family and friends — can see right through an inflated ego, and they will turn away from you in a heartbeat if they sense that you're trying to get them to join something just to gratify your own pride. The difficulty is that you need them to hear that edification from others in order to establish your credibility so it's a test of your will and character to not turn around and let it all go to your head. My only recommendation is to have someone you trust make an unbiased assessment of you every few months, as needed. For me, that person is my sweetheart, Keri, and it turns out that the assessment actually happens more frequently than every few months.

The Geranium Effect

Another aspect of edifying your expert is what I call the "Geranium Effect." Typically, you've invited this person to come and present because he or she has specific knowledge to present about the topic. Once you've invited someone to present, you need to stay out of the way. The most common manifestation of this problem is after the event when you're introducing a guest to the speaker. You make the introduction and then what happens? All too often, your excitement bubbles to the surface and you start asking the presenter to talk about one thing or another. Then, even before the speaker is done, you're bombarding him or her with another question or asking for another explanation. Typically, these are questions and requests about things you personally already know but which you are desperate to share with your own guest. However, by being disrespectful and interjecting yourself into the conversation so repeatedly, you actually undermine the presenter's credibility. You are, in fact, de-edifying the speaker.

That's obviously not your goal, but in your excitement, that's how it comes across. To your guest, it appears that you don't really care what the expert has to say. You appear too concerned with jumping around between topics of which you are already familiar, rather than listening to the presenter and learning more. This shotgun attack gives the impression that your expert is really no expert at all.

What should you do instead? After you introduce the speaker to your guest, act like a geranium. Why? Because geraniums do nothing. They just sit there and soak up the sun. That's what you should do as well. You aren't there to be the expert, so get out of the way and be quiet. Rather than asking questions and prompting the speaker with topic after topic, you should make the introduction and then sit back and listen. This will not only demonstrate your respect for the speaker and your character as a human, but also reinforce the credibility of the speaker. If your guest feels like you to have no reason to interrupt, then your guest is more likely to feel that the speaker is telling the truth and reinforcing the idea that enrolling is the right decision. If you're doing all the talking, the speaker can't bring any influence to bear on your behalf.

Optimism

Another way you can edify others is through having a positive attitude. You have complete control over your attitude — though that might be a hard pill to swallow. No one can make you happy or sad or mad or glad. You get to pick how you feel and how you act. Remember, you are the master of your universe whether you like it or not.

Because your attitude is yours to control, you can choose to either be positive or negative. It's really easy to be negative. All you need to do is turn on the TV to fill yourself with negativity. The news rarely reports on anything positive, and even TV shows nowadays are dramatizations of the problems and heartaches of life. The default for human attitude is negativity. However, you don't have to follow the default. You can choose to be positive, and you can make that choice a reality for yourself and those around you.

I was at a presentation once where a man shared some statistics about optimism. He cited a study at the time, which I didn't write it down right then so I haven't been able to find the study since. In any case, the numbers are good enough, so I'm going to use them to make an important point. According to this presentation, you need a 3:1 ratio of positive to negative just to stay afloat in life. In other words, you need to focus on three positive things for every negative thing just to move forward. A 2:1 ratio is languishing. You'll have general malaise and feel like things aren't going the way they should. This is not a recipe for success. A 1:1 ratio qualifies as depression. When I heard that, I was blown away, but it makes sense. We're so programmed to see and accept negative influences that they out-muscle positive influences. Without a constant, overwhelming influx of positive influence, the negative will easily outweigh it.

If a 3:1 ratio is required just to move forward, a 6:1 ratio is required to flourish. So 3:1 is just surviving; 6:1 is thriving. Would you rather just survive? Or do you want to thrive?

Interestingly, for a successful marriage, you actually have to do more than just survive. A successful marriage requires at least a 5:1 ratio; otherwise, the negativity will erode the relationship over time. Is it any wonder, then, that so many relationships fail in this country when so many people are so focused on the negative?

• • •

Imagine, instead, what would happen if we all spent more time focusing on the five or six positive things. What if news channels filled the airwaves with all the good things going on around the world, like stories of people helping one another? What if political races were more about who has done more good and less about who has done less bad?

When we focus on the positive, our own outlook improves. Interestingly, your attitude also has a direct correlation to your health. Positive people are less likely to get sick and they stay sick for less time. Being negative increases your risk for cardiovascular disease and heart attack. Thus, one of the best ways to edify the people around you is to be positive.

We all know people we just love to be around because they always see the good in situations. They are like bright lights and we're drawn to them like moths because just being around them helps us feel better about ourselves. Usually, we dismiss their attitudes by saying things like, "I could never be like that" or "She's such a saint." In effect, we're trying to distance ourselves from that positive attitude and give ourselves an excuse to not emulate it.

The truth is, you can have that same kind of attitude with some training and practice. Changing your attitude isn't as easy as flipping a switch in your head, but it is as simple as following a few steps every day.

First, start off every morning by writing down a few things that you're grateful for, things that make you happy. It doesn't need to be a long list, and you should avoid writing the same things over and over again. Instead, write new things every morning.

Second, close each day by going back to that gratitude journal and writing, in detail, some good event that happened to you during the day. It doesn't need to be a big event (my spouse sent me a supportive text just when everything else was going wrong), but it can be (I finally landed that big promotion or deal). The key here is to describe the event in detail. Record your feelings, write about your surroundings, and talk about the setting and people involved.

● ● ●

These two, simple tasks will help you to rewire your brain to look for positive things in life. Thankfully, no matter how hard the world tries to make us think otherwise, there are positive things going on around us all the time. We just have to be open to seeing them.

Your Turn

And that's it. I'm done. You have now received a download of everything you need to be successful in our amazing profession. The only thing left to do is to get to work.

As you do, you'll notice that nothing I've told you is complex or difficult to understand, but that doesn't mean it's easy to do all these things and, most importantly, do them consistently. Like I said in the beginning, it's a simple business, but it's not always an easy one. Thankfully, it's a profession in which anyone can be successful. If you can guarantee to me your efforts, I can guarantee your results. That determination can only be made by you, so the guarantee is up to you as well.

You just need to find a product that exhibits the three essential traits and follow the vital behaviors. After that, it's just a matter of duplicating your efforts to duplicate your results. Everything else I've discussed herein is designed to help you refine yourself and improve your skills and bolster your success.

This chapter is yours and yours alone. Only you can make or break your success. The good news is that you don't have to rush out and convert the world all at once. If you'll just commit to the principles in this book and stick with them when things get difficult, you'll make it to the finish line.

I want to close with a story. It's a true story taken from "Think and Grow Rich" by Napoleon Hill, and it demonstrates how your dedication can break or make you.

● ● ●

An uncle of R.U. Darby was caught by the "gold fever" in the gold-rush days, and went west to DIG AND GROW RICH. He had never heard that more gold has been mined from the brains of men than has ever been taken from the earth. He staked a claim and went to work with pick and shovel. The going was hard, but his lust for gold was definite.

After weeks of labor, he was rewarded by the discovery of the shining ore. He needed machinery to bring the ore to the surface. Quietly, he covered up the mine, retraced his footsteps to his home in Williamsburg, Maryland, told his relatives and a few neighbors of the "strike." They got together money for the needed machinery, had it shipped. The uncle and Darby went back to work the mine.

The first car of ore was mined, and shipped to a smelter. The returns proved they had one of the richest mines in Colorado! A few more cars of that ore would clear the debts. Then would come the big killing in profits.

Down went the drills! Up went the hopes of Darby and Uncle! Then something happened! The vein of gold ore disappeared! They had come to the end of the rainbow, and the pot of gold was no longer there! They drilled on, desperately trying to pick up the vein again – all to no avail.

Finally, they decided to QUIT.

They sold the machinery to a junk man for a few hundred dollars, and took the train back home. Some "junk" men are dumb, but not this one! He called in a mining engineer to look at the mine and do a little calculating. The engineer advised that the project had failed, because the owners were not familiar with "fault lines." His calculations showed that the vein would be found JUST THREE FEET FROM WHERE THE DARBYS HAD STOPPED DRILLING! That is exactly where it was found!

The "Junk" man took millions of dollars in ore from the mine, because he knew enough to seek expert counsel before giving up.

Most of the money which went into the machinery was procured through the efforts of R.U. Darby, who was then a very young man. The money came from his relatives and neighbors, because of their faith in him. He paid back every dollar of it, although he was years in doing so.

Long afterward, Mr. Darby recouped his loss many times over, when he made the discovery that DESIRE can be transmuted into gold. The discovery came after he went into the business of selling life insurance.

Remembering that he lost a huge fortune, because he STOPPED three feet from gold, Darby profited by the experience in his chosen work, by the simple method of saying to himself, "I stopped three feet from gold, but I will never stop because men say 'no' when I ask them to buy insurance."

Darby is one of a small group of fewer than fifty men who sell more than a million dollars in life insurance annually. He owes his "stickability" to the lesson he learned from his "quitability" in the gold mining business.

Before success comes in any man's life, he is sure to meet with much temporary defeat, and, perhaps, some failure. When defeat overtakes a man, the easiest and most logical thing to do is to QUIT. That is exactly what the majority of men do.

There's an interesting conundrum in our society today which tends to rob people of their success just as they are closing in on it. People, in general, think that failure is an indication that they've taken a wrong turn somewhere. If you fail to reach your grandmother's house, that may be the case. They think about success and failure in terms of this kind of relationship:

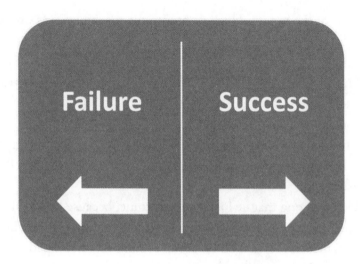

When it comes to success, however, nothing could be further from the truth. Think of people like Michael Jordan, Colonel Sanders, Benjamin Franklin, or Thomas Edison. All of them failed numerous times before succeeding. The reality is that the relationship between success and failure is very different from what people expect:

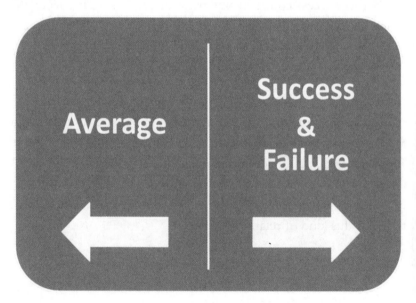

So look at your next failure, your next hardship, as a milepost on the road to success. You have everything you need to be successful in the networking profession; now it's up to you to get out there and make it happen. It's simple, but it won't be easy, so you can't be easy either. Stay strong and remember your "whys," and your success will be unlimited.

Finally, good luck and God bless as you move forward.

Happy Oiling!

Justin

Suggested Reading List

I've compiled a list of favorite books from my personal library that are perfect to continue your personal development. I present them here in no particular order and recommend that you read all of them and apply the concepts taught. Each one will enrich you and reinforce your drive to succeed.

Making the First Circle Work, Randy Gage

The Slight Edge, Jeff Olsen

Think and Grow Rich, Napoleon Hill

The 7 Habits of Highly Effective People, Steven R. Covey

The Richest Man in Babylon, George S. Clayson

The 21 Irrefutable Laws of Leadership, John C. Maxwell

Beach Money, Jordan Adler

Start with Why, Simon Sinek

Millionaire by Halftime, Presley Swagerty

Be Our Guest, Disney Institute and Theodore Kinni

Smart Couples Finish Rich, David Bach

Additional dōTERRA Resources

www.doterra.com

Corporate website with general information about dōTERRA.

www.doterratools.com

Tools and information to promote your success in dōTERRA.

www.doterrauniversity.com

dōTERRA corporate getting started program.

www.myoilbusiness.com

Support materials, tools and additional resources.

www.advocatewellness.com

Step-by-step training process on dōTERRA products and business, specific to your team, created by your upline leaders; video based.

Bonus Chapter – Diamond Tips

As we were finishing up the book, we felt it would be of great value to offer you some words of advice from some of our leaders. As we are never done learning, enjoy these tidbits of wisdom, as we have.

Stacy Paulsen - "I wish I had learned sooner that I needed to get outside myself! My biggest hang up was "me". When I forgot myself, my goals, my needs, my fears and truly sought to serve others, finding out their needs, desires and fears, that's when I began do something truly great. Fear is the #1 cause of failure and how do we counter this fear? I found that "Perfect love casteth out all fear." Serving others gets rid of the fear and tremendous results ALWAYS follow."

Shauna Wetenkamp – "Be solid in who you are, and if you aren't, be teachable and willing to learn more about yourself than you ever thought possible."

Jeff & Diane Shephard – "Learn how to teach an effective, duplicable class & then teach others how to do the same. Stay consistent. Decide NOW that you will reach your goals despite what disappointments may come. And, they WILL come! The best way to reach your goal is to help others reach their goal."

Jennifer Accomando – "Keep your presentations and teaching simple. We do not reinvent the wheel, we simply duplicate leaders, those who have successfully paved the way before us."

Michael Rothschild – "When you care about people, everything else will follow. Have confidence in our products, people and company. With doTERRA, this confidence is real and we can all have it. It has not been easy, but nothing really worth it is.

I want to send that message to everyone- we are all pioneers and have been given this gift to share. Just go out and share it- anything you want to achieve, will be achieved, in its own time. Just keep sharing. Never, ever, let other people's judgments affect your goal. Keep your focus."

Christian Overton – "If you can dream it, you can achieve it! Figure out your "why." Create visuals to serve as a daily reminder of your "why." Align yourself with only those people who will encourage and uplift. Work with those whom have had success and are willing to spend the time to show you how they did it. Invest in people and their needs. Help enough people get what they want, so you can have what you want. Therein lies the real key to success. Discovering what it is you want and working hard enough for long enough to get it. We have an opportunity to make a huge positive impact in our own lives, while helping others succeed. Does it get any better than that?"

Roger & Carol-Ann Mendoza – "The main ingredient that my wife and I have in building our business is to nurture the relationships with our leaders; become genuinely interested in everyone you meet without the intent of just enrolling them into our business. When they see you are interested in them, our human nature as friends will help them to be genuinely interested in who you are, and what you do. Create belief and confidence in everyone and you will see your business grow. Even if the person you meet never enrolls, you may have made a friend for life."

Scott & Rhonda Ford – "If we would have known, in the beginning, how well the compensation would be paying out, we would have shared the business a lot more than we did. But we didn't have anything to look up to. We were not sure this was even going to work. But we kept going because we believed in the products, the executives, and had passion to serve and share.

This business will not work without consistently sharing, enrolling and following up. Being persistent and consistent (through the ups and downs) has made this work and continues to make this work. Presidential Diamond is right around the corner because of these two attributes that we use as a daily routine."

Annie Clark – *"Be Kind For Everyone You Meet Is Fighting Their Own Battle.* I achieved my success by never expecting anything from someone else that I wasn't prepared to do myself. So first doing it myself, then assisting and mentoring my team to do what was necessary. Making that call to someone and asking them point blank to look at the company, and to look at it with me. It was action and perspective with my antennae tuned in to others needs, and meeting those needs."

Patricia Leavitt – "Having never been involved in MLM's before this has been a journey of courage, frustration, education, devotion, contentment, enlightenment, but most of all Courage.

Courage to take the first step. Frustration that the first step went the wrong way. Education when I learned which road to travel. The devotion I learned when following our fearless leaders. The contentment of knowing we are teaching and sharing with others, to change our lives. And finally enlightenment of knowing that I can continue to serve others and have the courage to do so. NEVER GIVE UP!"

Christy Hughes –"This business is not rocket science! It's actually *quite* simple. After using and falling in love with these incredible products, (and you will), it's almost innate to share them with others as you seek to help them with their health journey. You probably already know that you should educate yourself on oil usage, give samples, learn to do classes, and structure your team wisely. (Rinse and repeat) By that, I mean do it over and over, improving with time.

I'd rather talk to you about not giving up. The single factor that those who succeed and those who do not is DETERMINATION. Period. Yeah, some people have sales experience, or are prettier, or funnier. I've seen all types of people rock this business, no matter their background, culture, ethnicity, language, etc. It all boils down to really wanting to help others and showing them the way. Stay in contact with those who take a while. They will know that you are their 'oil person' when they are ready. Then it becomes amazing to see lives literally changed by what you shared with them. *That's* empowering. This works. You can do it. It's worth it."

Jason & Sharon McDonald –"KEEP IT SIMPLE! Live moving forward, learning from your experiences and not looking back at your regrets. Build community EVERYWHERE you go. Be HUMBLE! Build to that Power of 3 $250 bonus, teaching everyone the same. Your reward will come."

Tammy Stephens – "Get yourself out of the way and find out what others want by asking good questions. Once you've done that, meet people where they're at, letting them proceed at their own pace. Then based on what people do, not what they say they will do, invest your time and resources into those ready to work now."

Gerard Tehoti –"Pay attention to the little details and believe in yourself, healing begins with you. dōTERRA has given me the opportunity to heal physically and financially. It will duplicate when it's done from the heart."

PJ Hanks – "After four years of building my dōTERRA business I have come to look for words of inspiration from others to help guide me in my choices. I have a list of the ones that have carried me, guided me, and inspired me."

"Keep growing and great things will come." *Natalie Goddard* (Believe in the process and just keep working and enrolling.)

"Don't lose momentum." *Emily Wright* (Don't slack off or it will be hard to get back what you have gained.)

"Courage is being scared to death—but saddling up anyway." *John Wayne* (Face your fears.)

"A raising tide rises all ships." *Dave Stirling* (If you help improve others regardless of who it benefits; all will benefit, including yourself.)

"Get all the way in the boat." *Unknown* (Commit to do it 110%.)

"The power of daily actions compound over time." *Unknown* (Remain consistent and optimistic and by all means, be persistent.)

"Each friend represents a world in us, a world possibly not born until they arrive." *Anais Nin* (Share, share, share and your friends will become endless.)

"Don't just sit there and complain, do something." *PJ Hanks* (Learn to replace complaining with making requests and taking action that will achieve your desired outcomes.)

Cherie Burton – "In dōTERRA, we are in the business of building *relationships*. Fostering the skill-set to talk with people, listen to and love them is at the heart of success in not only building this business, but in building YOU. I love that dōTERRA's culture supports personal growth and development through a service and sharing model. Confidence and success are created by simply showing up and connecting with people, over and over again. If you consistently connect with others, from a genuine place of caring, you will have followers. And not just any followers, but those who've hitched to your wagon because you are a constant, caring presence in their lives, committed to their growth and well-being. People care less about how knowledgeable you are about oils and natural health; they are more impressed by your ability to make themselves and their loved ones feel valued and inspired. I love being in the business of building relationships!"

Rob Wilson – "Your level of success is directly linked to how much you believe in the oils. When you know that something will work, there will be nothing that holds you back from sharing them with everyone. Start out by educating yourself and incorporating them into your daily life. When you are ready to share, do so with an attitude of giving. Share because you want to help. Share because you know that these oils have changed your life, and they will change the lives of those around you.

When your business begins to grow, make sure to set up guidelines so it doesn't become all encompassing. Create a schedule that allows you to balance both your home life and your work life. Just because you are lucky enough to work from home, doesn't mean you should always be working at home. Find the right balance between work and family, and stick to it. This may not be a nine to five job, but it still requires you to put in regular work hours. Finally, always be grateful for the people that you get to work with. Never forget that your success comes not from just your hard work - but from the work of your team members. Love them, respect them, and be grateful for them. They are the key to long-term success."

Marty Harger – "Simplify! I used to think I had to become an oils expert and come up with new and different programs for my team all the time. Not true! Don't waste time reinventing everything (especially those of you creative types!) Use the plentiful resources we have to share oils successfully with others. Remember that 95% of the people you meet have no clue about essential oils. No matter how much you personally learn about them or aspire to know, they just need the basic info. Don't frighten people off with too much detail or freaky enthusiasm. Be real! Be normal! Remember to KEEP IT SIMPLE when you explain how they can get started with the oils in their lives and homes. This is not only the best way to build a

• • •

thriving business, but it is critical if you really want to help people. You know these oils work! Encourage people to take a step in a natural direction for their health and well-being, as you have. Be empowering. Point them to a few great resources available for them to get answers vs. trying to be their go-to expert. Keep the business story simple too. Don't assume they aren't interested. Assume they want to hear how they can pay for their oils merely by helping another few families to get oils in their homes as well. Keep it simple to learn. Simple to do. Simple to teach. That will serve you well and take you (and them) to the top!"

Dena McCaffree –"NEVER JUDGE! One day while cleaning my house, I decided to buy the car I had been thinking about for six months. I just threw my check book in my back pocket and went to the dealership. Evidently, I didn't look like I could afford to buy a car and was treated badly and looked down on. Did I buy the car? NO!"

Gale Sandgren – "Consistency and patience are probably the most important attributes required. Once you begin, it isn't a good idea to 'take a break' until you have enough momentum to do so. I've seen cases where individuals begin building their business, something happens or it gets too overwhelming, and they feel they need a break from things. Then, upon their return, they find it's much more difficult to get others involved. EVERYTHING duplicates.

Patience is required because we are dealing with people after all. I heard it once said by someone that building a network marketing business is like herding cats. I thought this amusing yet some days do feel a bit as though that's true. So, I just smile, and move on."

Peggy Smith –"Never let anyone determine your SUCCESS! You decide in your journey where you will go. Take care to help everyone along the way, we are never alone when we have like-minded people with us. You are the CEO of your company!"

Acknowledgments

To my sweetheart Keri, the deepest gratitude and appreciation for sticking with me and believing in me. To my parents for lighting the fire of entrepreneurship within me. To the owners of dōTERRA for having a vision bigger than any one of us and a mission of service and healing. To all of the dōTERRA family, for allowing us to be better people because of our friendship with you. Special thanks to the many coaches and mentors in my networking journey, your wisdom has made all the difference. Last but certainly not least, I would like to thank God, our Heavenly Father. Anything achieved in my life is due to His love.